IN
THE
PRESENCE
OF
GOD

IN THE PRESENCE OF GOD

Meditations

With Christ

on the Divine

Indwelling

CLARENCE J. ENZLER

This book belongs to:

Jehane Jones

Dimension Books • Denville, New Jersey

Published By Dimension Books
Denville, New Jersey

To my wife, Kathleen

CONTENTS

A man when he is born
is only a man.
But a man when he is reborn
is more.
He is a new man
with a new life
and a new name,
Christ-ian.

And he can say:
"I live now, not I,
but Christ lives in me.
But Christ is God,
and it follows, then —
GOD LIVES IN ME!"

I / THE PROMISE

GOD'S GIFT

*"If only you recognized
God's gift..."* (John 4:10).

In other conversations I told you what it means to be a Christian. It means being born again, so that you become a new person. It means being identified with Me, so that I live in you; and though I am I and you are you, yet we are one—one mystic Christ. To be truly a Christian is to become My other self.

Now I want to tell you about a gift I wish to give you; a gift which will make you more completely a Christian, and therefore more fully My other self.

This gift I bestow on My saints and they hold it precious. It is a key to greatness. I want you to have it, too, for you also are marked for the one true greatness which is holiness.

My gift, if you fully accept it, will change your life.

It will bring you peace—a serenity that all the world's turmoil cannot take away.

It will give you confidence—for you will place all your problems, your troubles, your ambitions in My hands.

It will free you from worry and fear, from greed and selfishness.

It will help you do the special work I am going to ask of you.

It will make you My happy one, because you will be My holy one, My saint.

— — — —

Are you curious about it; do you want to know what My gift is and why I offer it to you?

What is My gift?

It is the privilege of *habitually living "in the presence" of your God*. It is the continuous, loving awareness that the God of might and power, the God of all creation, Father, Son, and Holy Spirit, dwells in you. How this can be you will see later.

Why do I offer it to you? Because, as I told you, you are called to be My holy one. And in the work I am going to give you, you will have much need of it.

— — — —

What do you think of modern man, you who are My other self? Do you think that he is far removed from the savagery that debased him two thousand years ago? Then consider this. Herod's slaying of the male children in and around Bethlehem was a deed so monstrous that 20 centuries later you still recoil from the thought. But does Herod's crime compare in calculated, sustained, and savage depravity with the mass murder of millions at Dachau, Belsen, and Auschwitz? Do you see a similarity between the murder of the innocents, the slaughter in the concentration camps, and abortion for convenience?

Two thousand years ago human society was hard and cruel at the top and bitter and full of hate at the bottom. Is it really different today—not only in far' off places, but in your own city, your own neighborhood?

Two thousand years ago man made gods of graven idols. Today he makes gods of wealth, power, and pleasure. See how he grovels at the altars of Sex and Success.

Two thousand years ago the aristocracy among men dreamed of a self-created Utopia. Today man still deludes himself that by his own efforts he can build an enchanted society and achieve pure bliss.

Two thousand years ago man in general did not know his Maker. Today he is even worse off; he has dismissed his Maker.

There is a tumor in the brain of modern man which makes him a fool, saying "I need no God."

— — — —

Twenty centuries ago, when the Divine Wisdom decreed that the fullness of time had come, the Son of God became the son of man.

I came to change hearts, to overturn the way men thought, to reveal the truth that would set men free.

I asked the proud to learn humility; tyrants to learn mercy; the passionate to learn self control; the greedy to learn generosity; the easily angered to learn patience; the violent to learn serenity; the hard of heart to learn tenderness; the rich to learn the spirit of poverty.

I came to bring man the fullness of life.

I came to show you how God would live if He were man.

To many, what I asked was unthinkable, and they rejected Me.

Others, however, accepted Me as the Way, the Truth, and the Life. And there *was* a new life and a new truth and a new way of living, less complete than I wished, but still an immense change.

Now the pendulum has swung again. Man has again fallen into slavery and idolatry. Now men speak of a post-Christian era, as though the life and the truth and the way I brought were dead.

Are they dead? Are *you* dead? No, for I live in you.

But I must live in you more fully.

The Christ-life must be made new again, so that there will be a fresh conversion, another change of hearts, another overturning of the way men think and act, another birth of freedom.

I have chosen you, like another Paul, to be one of My instruments in this renewal of life. According to your abilities and circumstances, you are to bring My name and My truth once again before men.

Whether you are to be My apostle to the multitudes, in travel to far places, in preaching and writing, in persecution and torment; or whether your apostolate will be to the intimate few in your own circle, a teaching more by example than by words and done in relative tranquility, is for Me to decide.

Whatever your apostolate, however, you must begin by letting Me liberate you from the grip of passion and pride even as I did for Peter and John. You must help Me extract from you the venom of selfishness, and allow Me to plant and bring to flower in you, as in willing soil, the seed of true life, which is love.

Only then will you be able to reveal Me in this new age—because you live in Me and I in you. Only then will it again be said, "See these Christians, how they love."

Your task will not be easy. No, I tell you what I told My apostles: Men may persecute you just as they persecuted Me. Assuredly they will pay no more attention to your words than they did to mine. And the time may come when anyone who knocks out your teeth, who jails you, yes, even kills you, will claim he is doing right.

To survive these trials you will need My gift. By yourself, you will never be able to fulfill what I ask of you—to renew life—to help build a changed society on which My Father can smile. To live like another Peter or John or Paul—no, more, like another Christ—you must draw strength from My presence.

Ask no more why I offer you My gift. Now you know.

WISDOM BEYOND PRICE

"Give me wisdom..." (Wis. 9:4).

What are you thinking! "Lord, I know already that all things exist because of You, and that You are in them by your power, and that no man can do anything except You permit it?"

It's not enough. This is far from being *aware that I live in you.* It does not leave Me free to do for you all that I wish. To the extent that you ignore Me, you tie My hands.

But if you continually and lovingly recognize My presence, I will be intensely active in you and indescribably generous to you. You will know what it means to love your God and to be loved by Him.

This is what I offer you, My other self. Do not imagine that you can demand it, earn it, seize it, or buy it. No. But you can *want* it. And this is all I ask. From you whom I have chosen, should I be satisfied with less?

What does it profit a person to scurry about chasing after life's gewgaws as though these trifles were worthy of his whole concern? What does anyone gain by plunging himself totally into business, desperately pursuing ambition, chasing wild-eyed after pleasure, when all these things which promise to taste so sweet will eventually become like ashes in his mouth?

Does anyone live his life more fully by shutting Me out of it?

You know better. It is shutting Me out that makes a man dissatisfied, cross, impatient, a bundle of nerves—and sometimes it turns him into a self-centered, stingy, cruel miser, never realizing that he possesses nothing of lasting value.

For the poor who cannot see where their next meal is coming from, there is some excuse for being absorbed head over heels in getting a little ahead. But what excuse have you? Can you name one?

If you were continuously and lovingly aware that I dwell in you, how much richer your life would be!

My saints, I told you, held this gift precious. Let some of them explain why.

Is your work such drudgery that you shirk its responsibilities? Do you hate it so much it sets your teeth on edge? Listen: "Most of the failures of good people in the discharge of their duties come because they do not keep themselves sufficiently in the presence of God" (Francis de Sales).

Have you little self control? Do you despair of ever improving? "All sins are committed because we do not think of God as really present, but imagine Him as very far off" (Teresa of Avila).

Is your life without purpose so that each day leaves you bored and depressed? "It is always springtime in the soul united to God" (The Cure of Ars).

Do you fear old age? Do you dread cancer? Do you shrink from your inevitable death? "Even though I walk in the dark valley I fear no evil; for you are at my side (Ps. 23:4).

Are you destroying yourself with self-seeking? Do you find it terribly hard to love others as you do yourself? Listen to Me, My chosen one. "Come to Me. Love one another as *I* have loved you."

To be aware that I dwell in you will make you selfless. You

will understand that I dwell not only in you but in others also, and that in serving them you serve Me; and then your service and self-sacrifice will become perfect joy.

Ah yes, listen, My other self. How much richer, indeed, every moment of your life would be if you were aware with an unshakable realization that the Son of God dwells in you; differently, yes, but nevertheless as truly as He dwells in the bosom of His Father.

This wisdom beyond price, the knowledge that I not only behold you, but that *I live in you;* this I offer you, this I plead with you to accept.

I want you to be aware that through My Spirit I counsel you, teach you, direct you—but above all, that I myself live in you.

Because I live in you I do not invite you any longer merely to walk in My footsteps. This is appropriate for those who seek Me. But for you whom I have chosen, it is far too little. You must become continuously and lovingly aware that *I Myself walk within you.*

Because I live in you, I am not merely a Model for you to mirror, a Portrait for you to copy, a Statue for you to reproduce. No, I am much closer to you; the Statue leaves its pedestal, the Portrait its canvas, the Model His pose and entering into you is more you than you are yourself.

We are one; one mystic Christ. *And you are to be aware of our oneness.* This is My gift. It is yours on only one condition: You must want to receive it.

Want it, My other self! Desire it! Long for it! And you shall have it.

BE MY SAINT

"Your ways, O Lord, make known to me..." (Ps. 25:4).

This loving awareness that I offer you, I repeat, is not an end in itself. Its purpose is to help you rise above your natural limitations and become more perfectly another Christ.

Do you know what this means: To be another Christ? It means ascending to a new level of life. It means being one with Me in expressing the divine love to all men. It means joining yourself to Me in a unique unity to establish My Father's kingdom on earth. It means helping Me to transform the world.

This is your most demanding challenge, your fullest development, your noblest work, your highest success.

Do you want to be another Christ? If you really do, nothing outside of you can prevent it. Oh, yes, you will surely have trials; but instead of weakening you, they will build your strength. You will be tested; but every test will cement our oneness. Only one thing can prevent your becoming more fully My other self: If you refuse it; if you turn your back on My gift.

You have My pledge for this.

Does it seem too good to be true? How is it possible, you ask, that I have called *you* to such oneness with Me? Others, yes, great saints of the past, but not you.

Listen! I have invited *you* to so close a union with Me that only a great saint can achieve it. And the invitation itself *proves that you* can achieve it.

Never do I call anyone in vain. Never from the beginning of time has anyone been urged to love the Lord, his God, with his whole being and been denied the means. If you, even once, have felt impelled to surrender yourself totally to Me—and you know you have—then be sure that I have invited you to be one with me.

"But, Lord, I make no progress," you say. "Why do I fall so far short of what You desire for me; and, yes, what I desire for myself?"

Don't you know? Where you fail is in holding back part of your will. An alcoholic takes the first big step toward conquering his sickness by admitting with full conviction: I *am* an alcoholic, and I *want* to overcome it.

You will take an immense stride toward oneness with Me

when, with all your heart, you say, *"Yes, My God, I want to be your holy one."*

So many put this off so long. How often have you plunged yourself into business or pleasure, saying like Augustine, "Not yet, Lord, not yet?"

There is one simple difference between My great saints and the rest of men. The saints hear My invitation and they accept it, *totally.* And then, almost before they know it, they find themselves caught up in My presence, so that whatever they do they do with Me.

This is where you fail. When you pray, you seek not your own will but Mine. But when you stop praying to go to your work or your play, you seek not so much My will as your own. You pray to please Me. But you work and play to please yourself.

But the saints, ah, they go from prayer to work and from work to play and from play to prayer and it is all one; all My will, with theirs simply united to it. They try to desire nothing but what I desire for them; they try to refuse Me nothing that I ask of them. They do not turn away from any trial that I send them. They lose themselves in Me—only to find Me in them.

Thus they are always with Me—and I with them—not doing this or that so much as doing My will, which happens to *be* doing this or that. They act as they act, speak as they speak, think as they think because at that precise moment this is what I want of them. And the more they do this, the more My presence becomes real to them. Eventually, they live in a continuous, loving awareness of Me. And they become wholly My other selves.

But you hold back. You give Me part of your will, not all of it. You try to bargain with Me.

"Lord, make me holy," you say, and think you mean it. Perhaps you even tell yourself, "I want to convert whole nations like Francis Xavier. I want to preach Your truth like the golden-tongued John Damascene. I want to write profoundly on mystical prayer like Teresa of Avila, reform the world like Ignatius Loyola, be a great social worker like Vincent de

Paul."

You are willing to be a saint if you can be like one of these. You seek the impossible.

You can never be another Christ on your own terms. You will be fully My other self only if you follow My design for you, step by step, abandoned to My will, seeking to desire nothing that is not part of My plan for you, refusing nothing that is.

What is My plan? What do I want of you? Must I tell you? Don't you know that all I want is that you should live in My presence here and now, in this land, in this community, following the particular career to which you are called at this moment, satisfied with the emotional, mental, and physical characteristics I have given you, accepting whatever joys or sorrows I permit to come to you, full of humble wonder that your God is so interested in you; grateful in short to be completely YOU.

Face up to the world in which you live; face up to the challenges it presents. Accept your uniqueness; accept yourself.

To be content to be wholly you for My sake is the first step to becoming a holy you.

Learn this well, My other self; You can never be *a* saint; you must be uniquely *My* saint—or no saint.

You need be not at all extraordinary in your external life. Others may seem to be more devout than you, more penitential, more generous, more active in parish and community affairs, more successful in fulfilling the duties of their state of life. You may even be criticized, perhaps justly, for your failures in these areas

What is extraordinary will be within you and therefore invisible to anyone but Me: Your living in awareness of the God of life and love; your constant referral to Me of all that you do; your humble and complete dependence on the Holy Spirit to guide you; your total self-surrender to the Father in imitation of My total self-surrender to Him.

Do I ask too much? It is but a trifle for a reward so rich. Give Me your will, your *whole* will, and it becomes My solemn duty to protect and guide and care for you. All the power of the Godhead, I promise you, will then be set in motion to make you great among men, to make you another Christ, to make you My other self.

GIVE ME YOUR SELF

". . . stir into flame
the gift of God . . ." (2 Tim. 1:6).

Worldly ones will scoff. What I ask of you is too hard, they will say, or it is impractical, or it is out of date.

But even by worldly standards, the way of the world is the way of a fool. Only a fool gives up a supreme treasure for trifles.

I offer to make you so intimately aware of the living God that you will enjoy here and now a foretaste of the total joy that is destined for you hereafter.

Who but a fool would refuse?

True, you must renounce self-seeking; but this is to gain joy, not lose it.

You must give up some creature pleasures; but in giving up creatures you gain the Creator.

You must resolve to weed out of your affections whatever leads you away from Me; but this will make you richer, not poorer.

You cannot receive My gift if you set your heart on riches, prestige, power, pleasure, ease, popularity, or spiritual delight. So many do this. Poor souls! They think contentment lies in these things. Too late they learn the truth.

Be wise, My chosen one; shabby substitutes are not for you. You are made for God. Refuse to be satisfied with anything less than your God Himself.

Again I warn you that it will not be easy. To be another Christ is not for comfort seekers, lovers of ease, quitters, those who turn pale at the first sign of opposition.

It is for generous men and women who are humble enough to admit their weakness, yet confident that I will make them strong. This confidence gives steel to their spirits.

But while it is not easy to be another Christ, neither is it as hard as you might imagine. Do not be afraid. Surrender your whole being to Me. Put yourself totally in My hands. Once you take this first step, and truly this step is the most difficult, all that remains is serenely and peacefully to let Me shape you according to My plan. Soon in your work, your reading, your play, even your conversation and your meals, you will find your thoughts turning to me.

On all sides you will discover a thousand reminders of the presence of your God. The sun, the moon, the stars; a tree, a bush, a rose, a lawn; a lake, a river; a pebble, a grain of sand; a robin, a dog, a fish; a book, a song; a clear day, a rainy day: whatever *is* will whisper to you of its Maker.

Do you wonder what I want you to do with your life? In the tasks of the hour, in the circumstances of each present moment, you will recognize the whispered voice of the Holy Spirit. He will be your guide.

Do you ask how I want you to serve Me? In your fellowmen you will see Me. There is your answer.

Listen, and in your own soul you will find Me. And you will be reborn.

To take this first step of total self-surrender requires a certain boldness. You do not know how much I will demand of you.

Can you bring yourself to this total commitment?

Are you bold enough truly to will to be My other self?

Can you say to Me: "Yes, Lord, be it done according to Your word. I want to become precisely what You want me to be; no more, no less."

If you believe you can, read the Act of Self-Surrender which follows. Think seriously about it. Then, if you still wish to commit yourself, say this Act with deep devotion, and make it your own.

ACT OF SELF-SURRENDER

O Lord, God of Light, Life, and Love, eternal Trinity, I ————————, your servant, being in my ———— year of life, pledge to You anew my love and loyalty. I give you my entire self; my body, my free will, my spirit. Do with me exactly as you wish.

I thank you for giving me this present moment to know, love, and serve You. With my whole will, I embrace this moment in all its circumstances. I accept myself, my strengths and weaknesses, whatever I am, whatever I have. I accept my state in life and everything that it entails. Help me, My God, to live each present moment in your service, consecrating it to you with fervent love.

Without reservation, I now embrace also every circumstance of every future moment of my life; all that you have planned for me or will permit to come to me; every joy and sorrow, every triumph and failure, including the moment and kind of death that are to be mine. Your will be done. I accept it. I will it. I love it.

Further I offer you, my God, each moment of my past life. Receive now, I beg you, every thought, word, and deed which previously I failed to offer You or offered half heartedly. Even my failings, my refusals to serve, my betrayals of You, I hold up to You, God of all creation, imploring You to accept from me now the love I should have given You then. Receive now the changing of all my rebellions into humble, joyful, loving obedience. If You, my God, are eager to forgive me for turning my back on You and are quick to make good come from evil, as I know You are, will you not also transform my whole life into one continuous act of love for You? With You, there is no time; past and future are one with the present.

Take, then, my past, my present, and my future and fuse them into this one sigh of fervent love that is my desire. Make it possible for me to say in truth: I am Yours! Always I have been Yours! FOREVER I SHALL BE YOURS!

This is my earnest desire: To live in Your presence that I may serve You with gladness. Your presence, O Lord, I seek; hide not Your face from me!

"I praise You with all that is within me," says the psalmist. Who is within me? You, my God—Father, Son, and Holy Spirit. Let me praise You, then, through You and by You and in You now and forever.

Eternal Trinity, dwelling in me, accept my offering. Accept me. Strengthen my resolution. Help me to be what you desire, your holy one.

Omnipotent Father, all-wise Son, all holy Spirit, live in me! Act in me! Love in me!
So be it! So be it!

II / THE PRACTICE

HOW TO BEGIN

*". . . toward you, O. God, my Lord,
my eyes are turned" (Ps. 141:8).*

Now let Me show you, My other self, how to begin the practice of "awareness." The first step is to learn how to "place yourself" in the divine presence.

To do this, you have only to withdraw your attention from everything else and focus it as fully as you can on the Divine Being living in you.

Do you doubt that He lives in you? Then let Me say to you what I said to My disciples on the night before I died:

> I am in My Father, and you are in Me, and I am in you. If any man loves Me, he will be true to My word; and then he will win My Father's love, and *We will both come to him and make our eternal abode with him.*
>
> And I will ask the Father and He will give you another to befriend you, one who is to dwell continuously with you forever. It is the truth-giving Spirit...*He will be continually at your side, no, He will be in you.*

You have My word for it that I live in you, and that My Father and the Holy Spirit live in you, too.

Here is what you are to do. Every morning as soon as you are fully awake, reflect that the eternal, all-powerful, all knowing Divinity lives in you, and say something like this:

"Almighty God, I adore You. I worship your presence in the universe, and especially in man. I worship You living in me.

"I believe, Father, Son, and Holy Spirit, that you dwell in me. I do not understand it, but I believe it."

Then, if you wish, go on to say something like this:

"O Eternal Word, You who became the Son of Man, the

Christ, the annointed One, I believe that I am Your other self, identified with You in a mystical but real way. Live on in me. Help me to do what You wish, to speak as You wish, to love as You wish."

Let these sentiments come from your heart. Mean what you say. But while you are to be devout, fervent, even intense, try to keep your act of belief from becoming strained or forced.

This is all. This act is the core of the whole practice. Its effectiveness, however, will depend on the loving faith with which you make it.

In the beginning you will do this verbally, sometimes aloud, sometimes silently. Later you will often do it without words; by a prolonged glance or an interior look, much as lovers learn to communicate their affection by a gesture, a glance, or a gaze more eloquent than speech.

Note that you do not put yourself in the divine presence by merely thinking about it. No, you do it rather by directing your attention to your God in a loving, prayerful way. You do it by *intending to attend* to Me or to the Father, or to the Holy Spirit. You do it by opening yourself to an awareness of the divinity.

Are you curious about what happens when you place yourself thus in the divine presence? Perhaps you anticipate a vivid sensation of some kind, a strong "feeling" that I live in you and that an immense change is fermenting within you.

You must not expect to feel anything at all.

Your awareness does not depend on your senses or on subjective feelings of joy, well-being, or satisfaction. Do not seek, or even desire, any sensation that I am within or near you.

How then will you know Me? Will it be through a mental image of some kind? Again, no. The practice of the divine awareness is not an exercise of your imagination and it must never become that.

The way you will know Me is by faith. "Lord, I believe You dwell in me. Increase my belief. I do not ask to see or feel Your presence. On Your word, I believe it."

As is typical of the knowledge engendered by faith, your awareness will be indistinct, vague. With Paul you will see now "indistinctly as in a mirror."

Nonetheless, it will be real; it will be alive; and it will begin to influence your thoughts, your actions, your outlook, your whole way of living.

So now, My other self, begin. Simply withdraw your attention from all else and focus it through a fervent but calm act of belief on the Divine Being who lives in you.

GROW IN AWARENESS

*"Grow...in the knowledge
of our Lord"* (2 Pet. 3:18).

To "place" yourself in the divine presence is easy; to remain there is not in your power.

You can*not* accomplish it by resolving: All this day I will think of the Lord and I will be conscious of His presence.

Have you ever noticed when you were sick how impossible it was for you to pray fervently? Only by a special grace can anyone do this when he is in severe discomfort or pain. No more can you force yourself to be continuously aware of Me. Trying to do this will only make you irritable, nervous, disgusted or even rebellious.

You must understand that the habitual awareness of the Divine presence is a gift and you cannot take it by force. Francis de Sales used to tell those who came to him for guidance, "I do not say, be always attentive to God's presence, but multiply as much as ever you can the turning of your spirit of God."

How shall you do this? How shall you multiply the turning of your spirit to God?

By disposing yourself so as to grow in awareness. You will grow by responding generously to the desires I give you. Calmly recall that, in a way you cannot comprehend, the Divine Being lives in you; re-recall this often; and patiently and humbly go on doing this until I give you the continuous awareness you desire.

Though this takes some effort, just as it does to acquire deliberately any habit, it will not be too difficult if you really want to do it.

Often during the day make simple acts of attention. "Lord, God of all life, I believe that You live in me. Help me to *know* it firmly."

At first you will need to make these acts at set times or under given circumstances, such as before meals or coffee breaks, going up or down stairs, before or after telephone calls.

If in your work you interview many persons, resolve to recall the divine presence between each session. Ask Me to help you to be kind and wise, to make you see that I live in your fellowmen as I do in you.

If you work at a desk, you might try to form the habit of recalling My presence whenever you look at the clock or your watch.

If you read a great deal, recall the divine indwelling before every chapter or new subject.

This need not take much time; five seconds may be quite enough.

In forming this habit, resolution counts for much less than desire. When with a quiet longing you *want* to be aware of Me and to do everything in union with Me, you will find yourself flashing many quick glances in My direction.

Show Me that you want this attraction, and I will give it to you.

With gentle perseverance, then, continue your acts of belief, your quick glances, often during the day.

One thing that will especially help you to grow in awareness is speaking to the Trinity in frequent, simple bursts of conversation. Talk to the Father as to your father—He *is*. Talk to the Holy Spirit as to one who dearly loves you—He *is* the Spirit of Love. Talk to Me as to your other self—I *am*.

Talk simply, openly, as to one from whom you have nothing to hide and in whom you place all your trust; truly you can hide nothing, and you may rightly expect everything.

Speak about your work and your worries; your joys and disappointments; your trials and temptations; speak about anything. All that you do or think or desire is material for our conversation. No matter that the Divine Wisdom already knows it.

You wish to form the habit of living in My presence? Tell Me about it—"Lord, I can do this only if You make it possible —only if You do it for Me."

You are worried? I know you are, but tell Me—"Lord, I'm upset. I realize everything is in Your hands, but I can't help being worried. Help me, please! Increase my trust!"

You are distressed because you have failed Me in some way? "Lord, forgive me. I want to do only what you wish. Help me. Otherwise, I can do nothing but fail over and over again. Lift me up and hold me straight!"

On beginning your work—"Help me, Father, to do your will." In the midst of it—"Lord, I offer You this work as You offered Yours to Your Father when you were a carpenter in Nazareth." And when you finish—"Thank you, Holy Spirit, for assisting me; for making my work easy and pleasant."

You do not need great knowledge, or fine words, or lofty sentiment. You need only humility, sincerity, love.

Speak often and you will surely grow. Speak to your God directly in words; but speak also through your duties, your desires, joys, sorrows.

Your work, your play, your family, your community duties, will all be communications between your God and you. You will learn to see the divine will in all the circumstances and events of your daily life. "Dominus est," you will say. "It is the Lord."

Even in your most inconsequential thoughts, words and actions, you can discover overtones of the precious awareness of the Almighty.

Thus you will grow in awareness, slowly or rapidly according to how fully you respond to your desire and My plan for you. For weeks you may be aware of the divine presence only at wide intervals and then for just a moment. But only desire deeply and persevere quietly, and the time must come when your awareness will be continual, surpassing all that you dared to expect.

DEGREES OF AWARENESS

"...to be near God is my good" (Ps. 73:28).

To stay in My presence you do not need to be constantly thinking of Me. It is important that you understand this, My other self.

You must not try to remain aware of the divine indwelling by telling yourself over and over in an incessant refrain, "God is here," "Christ is here."

When you are with someone you love, do you keep reminding yourself, "My friend is here?" Of course not. You *know* it. So you speak, you listen, you enjoy your friend's company.

It is true that in the beginning, when you are first striving to become habitually aware of the divine indwelling, since you cannot see or hear or sense the divine presence, you will need to remind yourself at intervals. But do not stop there. Go on to talk, to listen, to enjoy My company.

Being continually aware of your God, then, is a state of being "pointed" in His direction, of being, so to speak, turned toward or "tuned in" to the Divine Being. It is this being turned "God-ward" that enables you to do whatever you do in union with Me.

Just as your awareness of those you love fluctuates according to circumstances, so your awareness of the divine presence will vary from time to time.

You know that lovers are sometimes so engrossed in each other that they are oblivious to everything going on around them. Sometimes when you are praying you may be similarly absorbed. Such total awareness is a special gift. No one has it always; only a few have it often.

Usually when lovers are earnestly and attentively conversing, they are still somewhat aware of what is going on nearby. Normally, when you pray you will still be somewhat distracted by what is happening around you or by the activity of your mind.

Sometimes when you are with friends your attention is rather evenly divided between your awareness of them and other demands requiring your partial attention: eating, playing cards, reading the newspaper, listening to music. Your mind swings back and forth freely between your friends and what you are doing. A similar degree of awareness of Me may be yours during much of the day.

Even when your duties require intense concentration, your awareness can still be maintained. Just as a lover, absorbed in some mentally demanding project, will stop from time to time to look at his beloved or speak to her or think of her, so you should do. No duty is so demanding that it compels your full, unremitting attention for hours on end. Your mind is incapable of such sustained concentration except under unusual circumstances, as in mystical contemplation. Even in your most engrossing duties, therefore, turn to Me fleetingly at intervals.

Finally, a lover is usually vaguely aware in the back of his mind that his beloved is near—in another room, perhaps—even though his absorption in some task prevents his thinking of her. You also can be aware of the Divine Presence at all times "in the back of your mind."

Living in awareness of the divine indwelling is not, then, a continual, conscious, and clear recollection that the Father, the Holy Spirit, and I live in you. Outside of prayer it will usually be a vague, indistinct "knowing."

Someone has insulted you and you are about to pay back the injury. Before a word leaves your lips, you are suddenly indistinctly aware that I wish you to suffer this offense in silence. You may have a vague inspiration to thank Me for letting you have the occasion to offer this sacrifice; perhaps, you will even feel kindly toward your offender for giving you the opportunity to bear this injury as My other self.

None of this may fully enter your consciousness. If someone were to ask you why you did not complain, you might be unable to explain it without first carefully examining your motives. This is living in My presence.

Sometimes when you anticipate a pleasant experience, such as a birthday celebration, meeting old friends after a long separation, or a big surprise of some kind, you have a vague "good" feeling all day long, even when you are not thinking about the joy to come. People notice it. They say, "You're happy today." So also an indistinct awareness of your God can fill your soul, pervading all that you do, making you "happy today."

As you grow, you will discover that some one of these different degrees of awareness can be yours at all times.

Try to anticipate the kind of awareness that corresponds to your circumstances. In your silent mental prayer or in thanksgiving after Mass and Communion, calmly seek to shut out all distractions so that if I choose I may render you totally recollected. Be *willing,* in short, to be absorbed by the divine indwelling. But do not seek it by any effort of your own; this is futile. Simply be open. Place no obstacle in the way.

In vocal prayer, especially public prayer, you must give attention to what you are doing. Do not anticipate deep recollection at such times.

In your daily occupations your awareness will be affected by how closely you must concentrate. In driving your car, for instance, most of your attention must be centered on traffic and the road. Your awareness may be similar to that which you might have of a friend riding at your side.

Look for the divine presence, therefore, in a way that is appropriate to the circumstances of the moment. Trust Me to know and provide the precise degree of awareness that is best for you at any time. You need only desire it and be ready to receive it.

OBSTACLES

"...for in fire gold is tested,
and worthy men in the crucible
of humiliation" (Sir. 2:5).

To form the habit of living in the divine presence you will have to guard against too much frivolous thinking, too many idle pastimes and conversations.

Recall what you did yesterday; the time you frittered away; the dozens of intervals when your mind was relatively free; walking along the street or from room to room, driving your car, eating, shopping, catching your breath between tasks, just sitting.

During all these intervals you could choose between letting your thoughts ramble idly about food, sports, clothes, gossip—or recalling My presence. You could decide to ignore Me or accept the favor of walking with Me as a continuing experience.

I do not tell you to *force* useless thoughts from your mind, nor that you should try to coerce yourself into a whole new framework of thinking.

Neither do I want you to be upset when you find yourself voluntarily dwelling on idle thoughts. It is not always easy to regulate your mind. But the more you do it the better it goes.

The best way to get rid of these useless ruminations is to let them fall from your mind as you might drop a few pebbles from your hand. Simply let go of them without effort. Drop them; don't throw them. As you form the habit of doing this, you will find your pattern of thought changing easily without strain.

Is this too demanding? Will you tell Me that you cannot use so much of your free time in this way; you need these intervals to plan your day, to reflect on your work, to consider personal, family, or other problems?

By all means, *do* plan; *do* reflect; *do* consider. If you are to be a "whole" person you must. These are not idle thoughts.

Indeed, the awareness to which I call you will help you to do with serenity what you now do with some disquiet.

Far from hindering your reflection and your work, your awareness will make them smoother, more effective, more satisfying.

You will consider your problems in a broader context, not narrowly and fretfully as you do now. You will view your day and your work not as isolated entities but as part of the pattern of your whole life. Relieved of the many trivial, distracting thoughts which buzz in your mind like so many gnats, you will plan and think with closer concentration.

You will accomplish more in less time.

So do not misread Me. I do not tell you to withdraw from your friends, to weigh every word you utter, to give up light reading, to forego pleasure. Not at all. You need recreation, amusement, and relaxation. Only give each of these a reasonable place in your day.

It is so easy to let them claim most of your life.

For example, how often you have set aside some moments for spiritual reading and, just as you were about to begin, you were tempted to glance through a newspaper or magazine, work a crossword puzzle, or see what was on television—to relax for "just a minute." And your curiosity was aroused, then your interest was captured, and almost before you knew it most of your allotted period for spiritual reading slipped away.

Or you were about to pray. Almost immediately your mind began to wander, dreaming about your future, reliving pleasant memories, thinking about your work, some problem, a bit of gossip, a show you'd seen, a friend you'd met. Perhaps you had resentful thoughts of someone who hurt, ignored, or ridiculed you.

As Augustine said, "...in how many tiny and inconsiderable trifles is this curiosity of ours daily tempted; and how often we slip who shall number? ...Our prayers are often interrupted and distracted; and though we are in Your presence, and directing the voice of our heart to Your ears, the great business of prayer is broken off through the inrush of every idle thought" (Confessions, Book Ten, XXXV).

You must put such intrusions aside. Even if they are good thoughts, they are worse than useless at this time. Bring your attention back to Me—gently.

Often you are distracted by a legitimate demand on your attention. But then, because you enjoy it, you prolong it needlessly. You turn from prayer or reading to respond to some demand, such as answering a question; but instead of merely answering fully and completely, you keep up a conversation of no consequence. Be generous with your time in serving your neighbor; be careful, however, lest you serve only your foolishness.

On the other hand, in your earnest search for the divine awareness, you may be tempted to fight against anything that intrudes on your attentiveness, even your responsibilities to your family, your work, your neighbors, or your community.

Certainly, you must not do this. These are duties. Rather than running away from them in seeking Me, you must learn to find Me in them.

DO NOT BE DISCOURAGED

*"Be patient, therefore,
my brothers..."* (James 5:7).

In attempting to live in My presence, you may encounter another kind of obstacle. Mostly because you want to go faster than I wish you to, you may grow impatient with your lack of progress. But it is not for you to say when or in what measure I shall make you aware of Me. Until you learn this, you will find the going hard. Your impatience seeks your will, not Mine.

Do not anxiously and continually examine your progress. Look at your dispositions, yes. Once or twice a day, certainly at night, look back briefly to see where you have succeeded and where you have failed. But do not try to "keep score" of your growth. Trust Me to advance you precisely as fast as is best.

Even when you find yourself straying from the ways I have recommended for becoming and remaining aware of Me, do not be upset. Say to Me, "Forgive me, Lord, I keep forgetting," and keep your inner peace. No matter how often you fail, simply try again.

Because I will test you to see if you are in earnest, you will need humility, perseverance, and above all, patience with yourself. Surely you understand that if I gave you the gift without difficulty to anyone who asked, it would be lightly regarded. To be habitually aware of your God is no small privilege, but an immense favor and you must prove yourself.

But all the while I will be helping you, watching over you, reminding you, calling to you.

I warn you that your efforts to live in the divine presence can become dry as a desert. Be prepared.

After months or even years of seeking and living in My presence, you may encounter periods, long or short, when discouragement will almost overcome you.

It is human to lose heart when you seem to be going nowhere —but you must never give in to discouragement. *Never!*

Again, let Me use the analogy of lovers. Sometimes one or both may be so bored or discontented that they can hardly speak. Perhaps they have quarreled; or perhaps, fatigue, disappointment, anxiety, or just feeling out of sorts is responsible.

If they truly love, they make up after a quarrel. If they are tired or in a bad humor, and they are wise, whether or not they talk about it, they make clear in some way that they are not disenchanted with each other.

You also may be bored at times, or tired, anxious, and so distracted that you may rebel inwardly against even the thought of recalling My presence. Your act of faith will seem a mockery.

Tell Me about it. No matter that I already know it better than you.

You cannot help your temporary disinterest. I do not blame you. Such a reaction is normal at times. Unless you clearly see that you are at fault, that you have caused it, you must not blame yourself.

Even if you are at fault, do not turn away. This is when you must live by faith and trust. Since this "coldness" seems to be My will for you at this time, say to Me that you want nothing else. Do this with as much serenity as you can achieve, and behold! in that moment your boredom and disinterest will begin to be dissipated.

Finally, beware of the worst obstacle of all: spiritual pride. Understand that the awareness of My presence is not a feat or an accomplishment for you to be proud of. Guard against smugness, against thinking, "I'm good at this," or "I'm better than others."

Such foolish pride forces me to take the gift away.

To be aware of the Divine Being is a grace for which you must be humbly grateful. Recognize your total unworthiness and the awe-full nature of the favor you receive. Like salvation itself, in Paul's words, "This is not your own doing, it is God's gift; ...so let no one pride himself on it" (Eph. 2:9).

Far from feeling proud, your very desire to live in the Divine Presence must be conditioned on My willingness to bestow it. Be ready to give it up, or even never to experience it, should this be My will.

To have such an attitude is to be perfectly disposed. Even if after having experienced the gift, you are deprived of it, you will not lose your serenity. Your faith will assure you that at the precise moment that is best for you, you must receive it again—and indeed you will.

JOYFUL SIMPLICITY

*"...rejoice, O hearts
that seek the Lord!"* (Ps. 105:3)

Are you thinking, My other self, that the practice of the divine awareness is extraordinarily complicated?

If you had to keep all these admonitions in mind all the time, this would be true.

But, of course, you do not. I tell you these things so that you may recall and apply them from time to time as you need them.

When you learn to drive a car, you are very aware at first of *how* to drive. You prepare mentally for what you are going to do. But as soon as you acquire some facility in driving, you no longer keep telling yourself to think of this, to watch out for that. You learn to drive better by *doing* it, not by *thinking* about *how* to do it. You focus your attention on the road and the traffic, not on what you are doing moment by moment.

So also you must focus your attention on the Trinity, on the Divine Being, on Me, not on *how* to focus your attention.

Never allow the practice of the divine presence to become a complex, joyless experience.

It is not complex, but simple. And the greater your simplicity, the sooner you will receive the gift and the closer will be our union. Joyful simplicity is to be your rule.

This is why I insist that when you make your acts of faith, you do so without force or agitation. Express your belief simply, calmly, serenely, confidently, joyfully.

As a flower gently turns its face to the sun to drink in light and warmth, so you should gently turn your face to the God of light and love to receive the increase of faith and the growing awareness of His presence that He pours into you. This is what I mean by being open to the divine presence.

There is no need to multiply acts of devotion. If you feel drawn simply to rest in the warmth of the Divine Sun, do so. This is precisely what I wish.

Indeed, try to preserve this attitude of resting, as if in the arms of your God, all through the day.

As you dress, do so calmly, putting no obstacle in the way of your peaceful awareness. Try to retain your calm restfulness at mealtimes so that in a gentle, serene way you may continue to be conscious of My presence.

In your spiritual reading do not greedily seek to devour spiritual truths as quickly as possible so that you can go on to another book and another and another. Your reading is to be done in an attitude of simple prayerfulness, letting the Holy Spirit inspire you through the author's words as He pleases. Stop as often as He moves you to do so and consider calmly what you have read and how it applies to you.

At Mass, realize that I am present in many ways; on the altar, in the priest, in the members of the congregation, in you. Look at Me in simple faith.

Especially when you meditate, try to maintain this simple, joyful attention. Such simple prayer is very good. Prize it whenever I permit you to have it.

Although I have told you that an excellent way to stay in My presence through the day is to speak to Me as to your closest friend about everything that occurs, you should not be always talking.

As you grow in awareness you will speak less but look and listen more. Our conversations will become a very frequent exchange of glances and eventually perhaps a simple, silent listening; again an "openness" to Me; a waiting, a resting so to speak on My heart.

Whether you work or play, read or meditate, eat or engage in other social activities, you will be united to Me by these frequent, simple, loving looks, without the slightest agitation or force.

In joy or in suffering, in tasks which delight you or fill you with distaste, in giving orders or receiving them, I will be with you.

Whatever happens the whole day through you will see as coming to you from My hand with love; and able with love to be returned to Me.

At night when you retire, you will renew your act of simple, loving belief, proclaiming your faith that the Tri-une God continues to live in you. Thus, you will offer Me even your sleep, taking your rest united to the Divine Being.

Joyful simplicity, this is the key.

Whenever you feel strained or agitated, smile at Me and I will give you the grace to smile at yourself. Say to Me, "Lord, keep me joyful. I want to go only as fast as You wish. Give me the degree of awareness that is best for me at this moment—this I want and nothing more."

The secret of acquiring a continual, loving awareness of the divine presence, in short, is what I told you in the beginning; joyfully and simply to surrender yourself so that I may give you the gift as and when it is best for you.

III / GOD OF CREATION

CREATION: INTRODUCTION TO GOD

"Will the saw exalt itself above
him who wields it?" (Is. 10:15)

Are you thinking perhaps that what I have told you is too simple, that I am urging on you the childish piety of a long discredited credulous age, concepts altogether out-dated in the "real world" of today?

It is far from that. Call it child-*like* if you wish; but remember, whoever does not accept the kingdom of heaven like a little child will *never* enter into it.

As for its being out-dated, how naive it would be to assume that the realities of life are hidden from their Maker.

This generation, My other self, which so prides itself on realism, actually has lost touch with reality. Modern man has plumbed the earth, the oceans, space, the human body and mind far deeper than ever before. What a pity that all this knowledge, far from sharpening his sense of wonder, has dulled it!

The more he learns about the *what* and *how* of life, the less he comprehends the all-important *why*.

Certainly, the scientific explosion is astounding to the intellect. But to leap to the conclusion that science can provide the answer to every human problem is to clothe science with a capacity far beyond reality.

It is unbelievably arrogant for modern man to refuse to admit, as in practice he does, the existence of any power greater than his own.

To make and regulate an earth, much less a solar system, still less a universe, is this humanity's boast?

Whence comes man himself? A seed fertilizes an egg and nine months later a baby is born; with arms, legs, eyes, and ears; with an instinctive ability to suck milk and a digestive system that transforms the milk into flesh, blood, and bone; with the latent ability to *think,* to *judge,* to *will.*

Did man say this is how it shall be, and therefore this is how it is?

There *must* be a power immeasurably superior to man's, and it must be actively at work.

What foolish self-glorification! that a man should think he knows the real world when he does not even know his own place in that world. A splinter in his finger is more real to him than the destruction of a whole city half way round the earth.

Man, viewing himself as the center of creation, as though all the universe revolved around him, is the victim of his own monumental hoax.

Look at the real world, My other self. It is from the real world, indeed, that you first learn about the power and majesty of its Maker. See what it can tell you about you and your God.

Have you ever tried to realize, what an infinitesimal member you are of the human family? If all of mankind now living were to parade before you in single file so that one person passed you every second—yellow men, black men, white men, mothers carrying infants, the aged in wheelchairs, the young bursting with vigor, learned professors and illiterate peasants, the rich and the ragged, the fat and the lean; if all these paraded before you, 30 years from this moment the first billion would not yet have passed your review.

Think of the billions now living, the more numerous billions who have lived and died, the billions yet to be.

Where would you find yourself among so many? Who but the all-knowing God *could* find you?

Let your littleness teach you humility.

— — — —

Though your senses bring you knowledge, they also deceive you.

Believe your senses, and you think you are at rest. Actually you are moving with the surface of the earth at great speed; if you are in New York, Madrid, Rome, or Tokyo, for example, at more than 700 miles per hour.

As an earth passenger you are racing around the sun at about 70,000 miles per hour. The solar system is orbiting in its galaxy faster than 500,000 miles per hour; the galaxy is rushing through space at an incredible pace.

In all these ways you are in motion; yet your senses would deny it.

You live at the bottom of an ocean of gases, a blanket of air which keeps the earth from becoming unbearably hot by day and frigidly cold at night. It provides you with life-sustaining oxygen, keeps your eyes from bulging out of your head and your eardrums from splitting. How swiftly you would die without it. Yet you seldom even think of its existence.

Intellectually you recognize that the sun's light and heat sustain life on earth and that coal, oil, grass, milk, and meat are all, in a sense, stored sunlight. But are you aware that the earth receives only about one two-billionth part of the heat and light emanating from the sun? One three-billionth and the ice age would return? Two two-billionths and the surface of the earth would be scorched? Can this be the result of an "impossible accident," like an ape sitting at a typewriter and pecking out Hamlet at random?

You know so little about the wonders that surround you; sounds you never hear because your ears cannot register them; glorious colors that are denied you because your eye cannot take them in.

Yet you are so proud of what you think you know.

Because modern man sends tiny objects into space, he boasts of exploring the universe. As well might he stand on the shore of the ocean, bend down and touch the water with his finger and boast of exploring the seas.

He isolates a virus, injects it into a cell, and calls this "creating." A mere seed has more life in it than man will ever create. Plant it, water it, place it in sunlight and it will germinate and grow and become food to keep him alive.

Did man give it that capacity? Did science? Accident?

Man is real and the world is real. But for man to live as though he were the center of the universe is to play the fool. To clothe his immediate world with supreme value as some do, to worship it in effect as the source of happiness, is to be totally deluded. The world has no such attributes.

Much that modern man presumes to call "real" is a figment. It never existed and never will. Modern man's conceit has cut him off from reality.

Yet he need only look at life to see reality and beauty and catch his breath in wonderment.

He need only stop before a tree and really look at it.

Why do you not open your senses to life: to a sunset, a water-fall, a thunderstorm, a flower, a blade of grass?

When you work in your yard or garden, why don't you pause to really see the trembling of a leaf, the hovering of a bee over a plant, the antics of a squirrel? Or the movement of your own hands as you pluck out a weed?

Have you ever really *sensed* the pleasantly warm sun on your skin, the breeze as it ruffles your hair? Have you looked at a flower with total attention and really seen its veins, its vivid color, and caressed its rich softness?

Look at the moon some night through the branches of a tree. Watch a cloud pass serenely over its gleaming face.

Instead of allowing the beauty that engulfs you to capture your mind for a brief enchanting moment, your thoughts are focussed on the humdrum. Your brow is wrinkled. You are tense. You worry.

What a sad thing it is to misuse the present moment. It is a lovely moment—this present moment—and you should be enriched and enlivened by it. It can introduce you to your God.

GOD OF SUN AND PLANETS

*"He stretches
out the heavens like a veil..."*
(Is. 40:22)

Scientists will tell you, My other self, that the age of man extends back toward the beginning of time one to two million years. How long is that?

You remember much of what you did yesterday, but only a little of what you did last year. Go back a hundred years and you did not exist; 500 years and the New World was unknown to Caucasians; a thousand and all of Europe was a feudal society.

But you would have to live a thousand years *a thousand times* before you reached the point at which, according to science, man may first have walked the earth. A million years! this is beyond your comprehension.

Yet before man came to be—I AM.

If you could take a million years and multiply it again one thousand times, you would reach the point, a *billion* years ago, when microscopic life emerged on earth.

Before the first amoeba ever was—I AM.

Five billion years measures the age of the solar system, and fifteen billion the beginning of the universe. BEFORE ANY OF THIS WAS—I AM.

Consider, My other self: This is reality. And this Ageless One—HE WHO IS—dwells in you. This also is reality.

— — — —

Meditate further.

Look toward the sun! Try to imagine what it means to be separated from that blazing star by 93 million miles of space. You cannot comprehend it.

Yet the earth, the sun, and the entire solar system are no more than tiny specks in the total universe. What then must you be? Less than a speck on a speck!

Suppose that by an act of My divine will I shrank the entire solar system so that the sun—that dazzling mass of fiery gases, so huge that a million earths could be fitted into it—became as small as a six inch ball such as you might easily hold in your hand.

The earth would then be the size of a bead, about one-sixteenth of an inch in diameter, revolving around the sun at a distance of less than 20 paces.

The moon would resenble a tiny grain of pepper circling the earth two to three inches removed.

Mars would be like a grain of salt 10 paces beyond the earth; Jupiter, a marble less than 100 paces from the sun; Saturn, a bit smaller than Jupiter, would be out an additional 70 paces or so.

Pluto, the farthest planet in the solar system, would be another grain of salt some four-tenths of a mile from the sun.

Such would be the dimensions of the solar system reduced 9 *billion* times.

Yet even in so shrunken a world, the universe would still be inconceivably huge.

Commensurate with this "tiny" solar system, how far do you suppose it would be to the next star, the one nearest the sun?

If you could stand in Boston, holding the sun in your hand, this star, another small ball a few inches in diameter, would be about as far away as London.

In reality the star nearest the sun is some 26 *trillion* miles distant.

Learn humility from your littleness, My other self. And begin to glimpse the power of that One—HE WHO IS MAKER OF THE UNIVERSE—Who dwells in you.

GOD OF THE UNIVERSE

*"...he himself made the
great as well as the small..."*
(Wis. 6:7).

Although the multiplication of immensity quickly becomes meaningless, I want you to peer still deeper into the Scriptures of the skies.

Astronomers will tell you that the entire solar system is an almost insignificant part of a galaxy containing more than one hundred *billion* stars, many of them far larger than the sun.

So huge is this galaxy that a light ray, traveling more than 11 million miles per minute, would take roughly 100,000 years to traverse it from end to end.

In miles, the figure is roughly 588,000—times a million—times a million again. Or 588,000,000,000,000,000 miles.

Even this galaxy, however, is but a speck in the universe— for the universe contains 100 *billion* other galaxies each comprising, on the average, some 100 billion stars.

Reflect on your insignificance, My other self. And on the majesty of that One—HE WHO IS—MAKER AND SUSTAINER OF ALL—who lives in you.

— — — —

Astronomers tell you that your galaxy in outline is somewhat spiral shaped and rather thick in the middle, a little like a grotesquely misshapen thick-hubbed wheel of a Conestoga wagon.

Suppose that the immense reaches of your galaxy were, in fact, so shrunken as to assume the dimensions of one of these wagon wheels. The entire solar system would then be about one two-millionth of an inch in diameter, too small to be seen through the most powerful microscope.

Imagine now a vast multitude of these wheels strewn in space, up and down and in all directions—more than 100 billions of them—separated from one another by an average distance of perhaps fifty paces.

Now for each of these 100 billions of wheels substitute the actual imensity of a galaxy—remembering that your own galaxy from end to end extends some 588,000,000,000,000,000 miles.

Utterly bewildering? Of course. How unfathomable to your intellect are the dimensions of the real universe!

— — — —

Yet HE WHO IS holds this universe in His will. It is His creation, made and sustained by His will alone. You might think of it as somewhat like a picture transparency projected on a screen. The picture exists on the screen only so long as the light continues to project it.

All of creation is sustained and continued in existence moment by moment by the Divine Light, the Will of that One —HE WHO IS—who dwells in you.

— — — —

Despite their number, the stars are lonely. The universe so swallows their countless billions that space is a vast emptiness.

Remember that the sun is a rather average star. Now imagine each star reduced to the size of a grain of sand—they would be separated by distances varying from roughly one to more than one hundred miles.

Think of a Sahara, or a Gobi desert, with each grain of sand in it many miles from the next grain. The awesome emptiness of space!

Are you not moved to say with the Psalmist, "O Lord, our Lord, how wonderful is Your creation!"—and will you not add, "How utterly insignificant am I?"

Yet HE WHO IS dwells in you.

GOD OF THE ATOM

"...you have disposed all things
by measure and number and weight"
(Wis. 11:20).

Even yet we are not finished.

A drop of water falls on your outstretched hand. You toss it off with a flick of your wrist.

In that flicked-off droplet, scientists tell you, are roughly 100 billion—billion atoms—100,000,000,000,000,000,000 of them.

Shall I help you see how small an atom is?

A moment ago you visualized the stars as grains of sand, some of them more than a hundred miles apart.

Think now of the atoms in a real grain of sand. Suppose that each atom were blown up, so that it became as big as the head of a pin. One grain of sand would then be about a mile long, a mile wide, a mile high.

The incredible smallness of the atom, you see, is no more comprehensible than the vastness of the universe.

But even as the Divine Being is the Maker and Sustainer of every star, so also is He the Maker and Sustainer of every atom. And HE DWELLS IN YOU.

— — — —

Inconceivably small as it is, the atom, like the universe, is almost entirely open space. If an atom were vastly enlarged so that its nucleus were the size of a plum, its electrons could be likened to bees flying around the plum half a mile away.

Moreover, like the stars, atoms themselves are relatively very far apart. Scientists sometimes compare the distance between atoms to that between the largest cities on the North American continent. Here at New York is one plum-bee complex, here at Philadelphia is another, another at Boston, another at Detroit, another at Chicago, and so on.

The drop of water you flick away, the chair you sit in, this book you are reading, the walls, floor, and ceiling of your room are in actuality almost entirely empty space.

How then, do they appear solid? This again is one of nature's wonders.

Each atom is a kind of electrical solar system activated by fantastic energy. In the hydrogen atom, for example, an electrically charged "something," which you call an electron, whirls around the nucleus 6,000 trillion times per second.

Not only is the atom in incredibly swift motion within itself, each whole atom is also moving with unbelievable speed within the substance which contains it.

This is why objects which are mostly "emptiness" appear solid to your senses—because they are activated by stupendous internal energy.

So empty indeed is matter that if all the space in and between each atom in the 555 feet high Washington Monument were eliminated so that only the solid matter remained, the result of this compression would be a structure smaller than an ordinary sewing needle. Yet not one ounce of weight or one iota of material in the Monument would be missing.

If all of mankind were compressed into solid matter, with all space in and between the atoms eliminated, the whole of the human race now living on earth could fit into the dimensions of a water glass.

You yourself, if all your "in between-ness" were eliminated would be submicroscopic. Your physical self in terms of solid matter is very nearly nothing.

Yet HE WHO IS dwells in you.

— — — —

Now finally, consider for a moment the wonder of your body. Science tells you it contains some 10 billion-billion-billion atoms—10,000,000,000,000,000,000,000,000,000.
They add up to a few pounds of calcium, enough iron to make a nail, sufficient carbon to provide several thousand sticks of lead for pencils, fat enough for a few bars of soap, phosphorus to make more than 2,000 matchheads, about two ounces of salt, a cube of sugar—and some 50 to 75 quarts of water.

Without asking your permission or even your knowledge, your heart pumps the equivalent of six barrels of blood every hour. Your blood stream contains about 25 trillion cells, each cell made up of a multitude of molecules, and each molecule in turn consisting of several atoms. Just as each atom resembles a miniature solar system, each cell resembles a miniature galaxy.

You do well, My other self, to marvel at your body. Yet is your spirit more wonderful by far. This it is that is made in the image and likeness of the Divine Being, with the capacity to will, to know, and never to die. This it is which makes you able to be another Christ, able to be My other self.

— — — —

Think, then, of creation, the universe, matter, your body, your spirit. Immerse yourself in the truth that the Divine Being is the ULTIMATE REALITY, that not one thing exists that is not of His making, not one event occurs except by His design or permission.

Meditate, and say with the Psalmist, "O Lord, my God, You are very great" (Ps. 103). And with the author of the Book of Wisdom, "You have ordered all things in measure, and number, and weight" (Wis. 11:2).

Yes, meditate, reflect, and lift up your heart in prayer.

O Maker and Sustainer of all that has being, who can begin to comprehend Your power, Your wisdom, Your majesty, Your glory?

God of the Universe and the Atom, all that You are is far beyond us.

How can man, whose life on earth is but a breath, gain understanding of your eternal NOW!

How can we, so small against the universe, even begin to fathom Your immensity!

Or how can we, so huge beside the atom, appreciate how You hold even the tiniest particle of matter wholly in Your attention!

How can I come to realize in even the smallest

degree the wonder that You assure me is true—that You dwell in me!

Am I important to You, O God? I must be; You tell me that I am.

Can it be, in this cosmos the dimensions of which shatter my mind's attempt to imagine them, that what I do matters? It must; You tell me that it does.

Is it true that You wish to give me the gift of awareness, so that I will *know* that You live in me, so that I can call on Your presence to release me from fear, to place all my cares in Your Hands, to taste now in anticipation the bliss I hope for in eternity? It must be; You have said it.

God of the Universe, God of all creation, help me to begin to understand.!

God of the Atom, You Who take such care of the miniscule, have care of me! Take pity on my dullness!

God and Sustainer of all that has being, make me see. Remove the blinders from my eyes! Take away my foolish pride, free me from illusion, give me sight!

Lord, that I may see!

IV / GOD IN HIMSELF

THREE PERSONS—ONE BEING

"Do we not accept human testimony?
The testimony of God is much greater"
(1 John 5:9).

Let us look now at the three Great Realities of Life: The Trinity, the Incarnation, and the Eucharist.

Which is better: to leave these impenetrable mysteries unspoken truths, or to remove the outermost veil which is all that words can do? Will partial revelation cheapen them in your eyes?

At no time in My mortal life is it recorded that I sought to explain any of these mysteries. I announced them, but I never explained them.

Yet, that you may come to know a little who you are and how your God dwells in you, let us approach the unapproachable.

Obviously, My other self, you can deduce something about the nature of the Ageless, Almighty, All-knowing Creator— HE WHO IS— from the universe and the atom. But if you are to conceive of the Divine Being as He is in Himself, you need a deeper knowledge than creation can impart.

Can you know Shakespeare as he really was—the living, breathing, thinking, laughing, frowning, happy, sad Shakespeare—from his plays alone?

Or Michelangelo from his Last Judgment or his Moses?

Can anyone truly know *you* solely from what you write, paint, or make?

Even if you could completely comprehend the whole universe—and not even if you possessed the accumulated knowledge of all of mankind could you do this—you still would not know its Maker.

Only God can truly and fully *know* God. "No one knows the Father but the Son."

Never in this life will you achieve a precise supernatural knowledge of the Reality Who is the Divine Being; yet you can acquire a valid, if extremely imprecise, knowledge of Him through concepts and analogies. And if you are to comprehend even a little how the Divine Being is present to you and how He lives in you, you *must* come to know Him better.

Understand, however, that any concept comprehensible to human intelligence is both explanatory and limiting. Human concepts may be applied to the Divine Being, therefore, in so far as they say in part what He is, but not in so far as they limit Him.

In My divinity, I am all that you can signify by the concept "being," but also infinitely more. I am all that you can mean by "life," or "love," or "wisdom," or "justice," or "mercy," but also infinitely more than you can comprehend. My Father is "Father" indeed, but not merely in the limited human sense. He is All-mighty, but He is infinitely more than an immensely powerful superman.

The Divine Being, in Himself and in His attributes, is totally without limit. Even this you cannot really understand, for the concept "without limit" is beyond your full comprehension.

Be careful, therefore, that in applying such concepts as "being," "life," "intelligence," "wisdom," "love," you do not construct a "divinity" made in your own image and likeness. Remember the words of Isaiah, "My thoughts are not your thoughts, neither are your ways my ways, says the Lord" (Is. 55:8).

— — — —

Who is HE-WHO-IS? He is A SINGLE UNITY and yet He is THREE PERSONS.

You say this makes no sense, and in human terms you are right. Yet it is the Ultimate Reality.

You know it is reality because, and only because, I say it is. That a Being of limitless power and wisdom, Maker and

Sustainer of all that has being, *must* exist you can deduce from observing the universe. But that He is Three Persons, yet only one Being, nothing in the created world could indicate.

Only because I revealed it could John declare:

"In the beginning was the Word, and the Word was with God, and the Word was God" (John 1:1).

And again—"there are three who give testimony in heaven, the Father, the Word, and the Holy Spirit. And these three are one" (1 John 5:7).

Only because of revelation could Luke write:

"And the angel answered her, the Holy Spirit will come upon you, and the power of the Most High will overshadow you. Thus, that which is to be born of you shall be known for the Son of God" (Luke 1:35).

It was to reveal the Trinity that I said:

"The Father and I are one. Who sees Me sees the Father" (John 10:30).

"When the Paraclete comes, Whom I will send from the Father—the Spirit of Truth Who proceeds from the Father— He will give you testimony of Me" (John 15:15).

"Go and teach all nations, baptizing them in the Name of the Father and of the Son and of the Holy Spirit" (Matt. 28:19).

— — — —

You say, "Lord, I believe this because You tell me;" but still you wonder: How? How can there be Three Persons—yet only One Being?

To you a person is a separate being. You are a person. Your best friend is a person. But you are two *separate* persons, and two *separate* beings, not two persons of *one* being.

This is how it is with man. Does it follow, however, that this is how it must be with God? Must a Divine Person also be so limited?

Because your eye cannot see in the dark, does it follow that nothing is there?

Because you cannot imagine the age or the immensity of the universe, will you deny them?

How can the tiny atom be so full of energy?

How can "solid matter" be a vast emptiness?

You accept these realities on the word of men. Is it too much to ask you to accept the Trinity on the word of God Himself?

THE DIVINE ACTIVITY

"... when things are in heaven,
who can search them out?"
(Wis. 9:16).

The riddles of the universe, My other self, are child's charades beside the mysteries of the Eternal God. You can no more pierce these mysteries than your eye can see where there is no light.

Yet, I say again, by means of concepts and analogies drawn from your own experience, you can *begin* to gain some insight into what your intellect can never comprehend.

Start with man himself. Builder, maker, producer of art, cathedrals, freeways, computers, rocket ships, you marvel at what he can do. But surely you can see that what makes these accomplishments possible is a greater marvel within him.

Man himself is immeasurably superior to anything he builds.

The fact that the author can plot a better book than he will ever write; that the artist can conceive a picture more beautiful than he will ever paint; the architect a building more magnificent than he will ever blueprint; the space engineer a rocket more powerful than he will ever build; all these indicate that man's act of thinking is greater than the thought he expresses.

Apply this now to creation. The universe, the "book" which God has made, tells you that HE WHO IS must be active and productive far beyond your comprehension.

But marvelous as is the universe, and man, and all created beings, they are limited; compared with the limitless Divine Being and His inner activity, they are completely overshadowed.

What is this activity which the Divine Being carries on within Himself?

You cannot expect to know this. Yet it is not illogical for you to conjecture, since you are made in the image and likeness of the Divine Being. Like Him, you have self-knowledge, self-consciousness, and the ability to will to love.

So we might ask: What do you do within *yourself*?

And the answer is that *you know and you love.*

Applying these concepts, then, you may say that within Himself the Divine Being *knows* and *loves.*

Applied to the divinity, however, such concepts are unutterably feeble. As the universe is in comparison to a house, or as the order of life is to the plot of a play, so the knowing and loving of the Divine Being are in comparison to your knowing and loving; indeed, the gulf is even wider.

Before you can know a tree, a rose, an animal, a person, they first must exist.

They *are,* and because they are, you can know them.

With the Creator, knowing a thing *causes* it to be.

To know a thing as man is to recognize its existence and some of its qualities. To know a thing as God is to *cause* its existence with *all* of its qualities.

All that exists came to be and remains in being simple *because* He knows it and wills it.

To use other analogies, you express your knowing in words and sentences. You say "apple," "orange," "snow," "New York," and each word stands for your interior conception of something existing outside of you. You "create" a concept and express it in a word.

Similarly, you "utter" your love in a sigh or a kiss. Your love is within you, but your kiss is its outward expression.

Applying this to the knowing and loving of the Divine Being, you might say that everything created is, in a sense, a "word" God has uttered. And all that is born of His love is His sigh or kiss.

You are My Father's word. *You* are His kiss.

These are feeble analogies and they may have little meaning for you. Do not be disturbed. One day you may know even better how weak they are; for I may give you contemplative insight as I sometimes do My saints. Then you will see and know these mysteries in a way you cannot even conceive of now.

But even after experiencing this insight and tasting this knowledge, you would still be totally incapable of expressing them.

Do not be upset, therefore, if these analogies have little impact now. What is vital is that you accept, on My word, the *reality* of One Divine Being and Three Distinct Persons of that Being.

ONE—YET DISTINCT

"How inscrutable his judgments,
how unsearchable his ways!"
(Rom. 11:33).

You can hardly wait sometimes to share a thought, a book, some news with your friends.

Even more demanding may be the urge to express your talent or skill. The true artist paints almost because he *must;* the singer almost *has to sing;* the poet feels *forced* to write; and each yearns to express himself to the peak of his ability.

So also, love demands that you pour yourself out in kindness, in giving, in bringing joy to your beloved.

Knowledge and love are outgoing. You know this from your own life.

Does it not fire your imagination when I tell you that your God is a limitless ocean of knowledge and love; and that His knowledge and love *demand* to be expressed without limit?

But nothing other than the Divine Being is infinite; therefore, His knowledge and love, if they are to be infinitely expressed, can only be so expressed *in* and *by* Him.

So it comes to this: The limitless divine knowing and divine love require sharing, they demand co-possession, they insist on co-enjoyment, *within* the Godhead, within the Divine Being Himself.

This deepest, most unfathomable mystery is the reality of the Trinity.

You may, if you wish, think of it like this. Within Himself, that is, within the ocean of knowledge that is His Nature, the Divine Being utters His knowledge of Himself. And this utterance is so perfect that It is what John was inspired to call the Word—a Person like to the Expressor, a Son begotten of a Father, of the same nature as the Father and equal to Him in every way.

That Person, that Word, the Word that was before anything was, the Word that was with God, the Word that *is* God—I AM.

Within the one limitless Divine Nature, My Father and I express our mutual love—express it so perfectly—that It, too, is a Person, possessing the full Divine Nature, just as the Father and I possess it, and, therefore, equal to Us in every way. This Person is the Spirit of Love, Love Personified, the Holy Spirit.

But how, you ask, can the Three Persons be equal? Since the Son is generated by the knowing of the Father, and since the Spirit proceeds from the love of Father and Son, does it not follow that the Father is greater, is "more God" so to speak, than the Son; and that the Father and the Son in turn are "more God" than the Spirit?

Why? Even among men, a son is no less human than his parents; he possesses the full nature of man just as they do. But the Son of God is not merely "son" according to your limited human concept. The divine "Son-ship" is infinitely more, for the Son is *one Being* with the Father.

Neither the Spirit nor the Word is less divine than the Father. The Three Persons of the Trinity do not *share* the Divine Nature. Each Person *possesses* It in its entirety.

But do you now say: Surely the Father must have existed before the Son, and the Father and the Son must have existed before the Spirit?

Again, why? Using weak words, you can say that the Father by His infinite nature always has been, and always is, begetting the Son. And the Son is always being begotten. Similarly, the Spirit is, and always has been, proceeding from the Father and the Son.

The generation of the Word and the proceeding of the Spirit are not in time but in what, for want of a truer concept, you call eternity; and eternity, as your philosophers put it, is an indivisible NOW ever standing still. Whenever the Father existed, the Son existed, and the Spirit also.

But is it not an impossible contradiction to say that Father, Son, and Holy Spirit are simultaneously one and distinct?

Not at all. They are one in that each Person possesses the entire Divine Nature in relation to the other Persons and in common with them. The Persons exist only in relation to one another; if one did not exist, neither could the others.

The Father cannot be Father without His Son any more than a man can be a father without offspring. The Son cannot exist without the Father any more than a human son can exist without a progenitor.

The Spirit cannot exist without the Father and the Son, for He is the expression of our love. Neither can the Father and I exist without the Spirit, for He it is Who unites Us in the one Divine Nature.

To put it another way, My Father possesses the Divine Nature only so as to give it to Me, His Son. My Father and I possess the same Divine Nature only so as to give it to the Spirit. The Spirit possesses the same Divine Nature only so as to unite Us as the One Being.

We are one in that we have one Nature which we fully possess in, through, and with Each Other.

But we are also distinct in that We each possess the full Divine Nature in a unique way.

What is distinct about the Father is to be *Father,* to give paternity, to possess the total Divine Nature in a giving way.

What is distinct about the Son is to receive *Sonship,* to possess the total Divine Nature in a receiving way.

What is distinct about the Spirit is to proceed from the Father and the Son as the expression of our mutual love.

The three Persons are not "in" God, as "parts" of the Divine Being. They ARE God. The Holy Spirit does not exist "in" the

Divine Being; He *is* the Divine Being. So, too, the Son *is* the Divine Being; the Father *is* the Divine Being.

Let Me say it once more: The Trinity is One Being, yet Three Persons. One, because the Three are identical in Nature and exist only in and through the others; Three, because each Person possesses this Nature in a distinct manner.

There are some who question the relevance of the Trinity. What does it matter, they ask.

If the knowledge of the Trinity were not relevant, would I have revealed it?

What does it matter, My other self? Listen.

But for the Trinity, your life would have no more meaning than that of a bird, a beast, a fish.

But for the Trinity, you could not be a son of God.

But for the Trinity, you could not live in Me and I in you.

But for the Trinity, you would have no pledge of your eventual face to face vision with the Divine Being.

As we go on, you will see this.

LOVE'S REVELATION

"Blessed are we...for what
pleases God is known to us"
(Bar. 4:4).

If you were to ask Me why I revealed the Ultimate Reality, the Trinity, I would answer: For love.

Love does indeed delight in revelation. It demands to express itself. And perfect love keeps no secrets.

So I disclosed this most sublime secret for love.

An artist shows his painting to the public; but for his beloved he must do more. For her, he must not only display his work; he must explain it; why he painted it; how it depicts his inmost thoughts, ambitions, dreams; the hidden meanings he put into it which the ordinary viewer will never perceive.

And his beloved, eager to know all this so as to understand *him* better, wishing to be one with him, hangs on every illuminating word.

Incredible as it may seem, My other self, your God wants *you* to know *Him* and this is why He reveals Himself to you.

Love prompted Me, almost forced Me, to disclose to man— to you—the inner nature, the inner activity, the family life, so to speak, of the Divine Being.

So that you might glimpse the immensity of your God's goodness and love, I had to show you that He is good not only in what He creates, but that in Himself He is goodness and love without limit.

And so I reveal to you a Father Who pours out His entire nature to a Son; and a Father and Son united in a love so stupendous that its expression is a Third Person equally divine.

Knowing this, you can begin to plumb the ocean of goodness and love that is the Divine Nature. Relate it to what you know of the love of man and woman, a love which pours itself out in an ecstasy of giving and results in a new human on whom the loving parents shower their tender affection—always recalling, however, that the life, the love, the joy, that man experiences are but droplets beside the mighty oceantide of life, love, and joy which surges in the Three Persons of the Trinity.

Now you see a little more clearly that wise, loving, and lovable as the Divine Being is revealed to be by the visible world, He must be infinitely wiser, infinitely more loving, and infinately more lovable within Himself.

How much more you should now know, trust, and love Him!

— — — —

There are other reasons also why I divulged the Trinity.

How otherwise could I explain Myself as the Christ? It was necessary to convince those who were to believe in Me that I am in one Person the Son of God and the son of man. They could see the humanity but not the divinity; I had to tell them about that.

How could there be a Divine Son of God unless there is a Divine Father to generate Him?

How could I make plain that My Father and I are one without revealing the existence of distinct Persons who are yet united as one Being?

How could I promise to send a Consoler Who—as God Himself—would enlighten you about all things, without revealing the Holy Spirit and His one-ness with the Father and Me?

To reveal Myself as I am I had to divulge the Trinity.

— — — —

Further, it was necessary to reveal the Trinity so that you, My other self, could know who *you* are.

Part of My mission on earth is to make it possible for you and all men to be true sons of God—and to understand your sonship.

The revelation that the Son of God and son of man has one and the same Father in heaven is the key to your own understanding that you also have a true "Father" in heaven. If I demand that you believe that I, Whom you call the Christ, am truly the Son of My Father—and I do—it is in part so that you may believe that you also have been destined from the beginning to be His child. Only when you see yourself in relation to the Trinity can you know your own glory!

— — — —

Finally, I made plain this intimate secret of the divinity as a pledge that someday I will introduce you face to face to the Father, the Holy Spirit, and My own Divine Person.

Even here in your mortal life I want you to know your God not merely as He shows Himself in creation, but somewhat as He is in His inner life; for only then will you begin to understand the wonderful joy in store for you when you shall meet Him in the life to come.

— — — —

Yes, My beloved, I revealed the Trinity because of love. In marriage lovers delight to share themselves as they are, mentally, emotionally, and physically in a sweet intimacy, so that nothing comes between them, nothing separates them, and they are as one. Among the proofs of My love for you is My beginning to show you the Nature of the Divine Being as He is in Himself.

The revelation of the Trinity baffles your reason and tries your faith. But, above all, it assures you that your God loves you with a triple love—the love not just of a Creator but the love of a Father, the love of a Redeemer, the love of the Spirit of Love Himself.

I GIVE YOU MY LOVE

"I will ask the Father
and He will give you another Paraclete—
to be with you always" (John 14:16).

Everything about the Trinity you must accept on faith, My other self, but especially what I now tell you. I am going to explain to you how "great" you are.

The ultimate measure of your greatness is that *you actually participate in the nature of the Divine Being Himself. You share in His life.*

When you offer a gift to a dear friend you sometimes say, "Take this, with my love." Really, the gift is only a token of your love. Your love is not distinct from you. It is an intellectual and emotional attitude and you cannot actually give it.

But as the Word, the second Person of the Trinity, I *can* actually *give* you My Love—and My Father's Love. For as I have told you, our Love is the Holy Spirit, Love Personified, a Person Who is one with Me and yet distinct from Me. And I can truly give that Spirit, that Person, to live in your spirit, so that you can possess Him, in a sense, as really belonging to you.

Again you ask: How can this be?

You recognize that there are different forms of life. The life of a plant is essentially its ability to take in nourishment and to grow.

The life of an animal is its ability to grow, sense, and act.

The life of a human is the ability, to grow, sense and act, but also to know and to love. These capacities are inherent in your human nature.

But there is also a far higher, above-human-nature—therefore, *super*human—life which you may enjoy as My gift to you: It is the ability to know and to love the Father, the Holy Spirit and Me in a superhuman way.

This, indeed, is the very life and inner activity of the Deity Himself—the knowing and loving of the Three Persons of the Trinity.

Your God allows you to participate here and now in His own divine life by communicating to you through faith a knowledge and love of Him. He gives you a foretaste of your future when He will permit you to know Him not in the dimness of faith but by the clear and direct "face-to-face" intellectual gaze of the beatific vision—when you will know Him and love Him and be united with Him in a way totally beyond your present comprehension.

Meantime, here and now, you can participate by faith in His own life; so much so indeed that He Himself lives in you.

But you ask, how does God, the ONE-WHO-IS, dwell in me? Does this mean that in giving me existence, He is *in* me somewhat as Michelangelo is *in* his David, or Raphael is *in* his Madonna?

It is immeasurably more than that.

Or does it mean that, since He gives me life, He is in me as my parents are in me?

Again, it is more, much more.

Though your parents passed life characteristics on to you by inheritance, and though they helped shape your mind and train your will, they have never lived in you or you in them in such a way that you actually *participated* in their life. No, not even when you were in your mother's womb.

But you *do truly participate* in the life of the ONE-WHO-IS. You truly live in Him and He lives in you.

The Divine Being is pure Spirit and you are part spirit. And Spirit can unite Itself to spirit in a manner impossible between body and body.

He Who is pure Intelligence and pure Love and pure Light can pour into your spirit His Intelligence, His Love, and His Light so that you actually participate in and share in what is His by nature—and He does!

Let Me be more specific.

On the night before I suffered I prayed to My Father, begging Him that the Love with which He loves Me might live in you.

But, as I have told you, the Love with which My Father loves Me—and the Love with which I love Him—*is* the Third Person of the Trinity, the Holy Spirit.

What I begged of My Father, therefore, was that the Holy Spirit Himself might dwell in you. And He does!

I promised you a Consoler who would teach you and guide you and live in you. And He does!

In times past one man would sometimes give another a slave to serve him. In a way that you cannot understand but that, nevertheless, is real and true, I give you My Spirit, not as your slave but as your Benefactor. Whatever you ask of Him, He will do for you.

He is yours to call on for inspiration, for strength, for joy, and peace, and charity, and all blessings.

Think of this stupendous truth, My other self. Meditate on it! Contemplate it! Believe it! Even if you were to dwell on it with all your powers of concentration for a thousand years, you could not begin to exhaust its meaning.

The very PERSON OF LOVE is at your call. HE LIVES IN YOU.

Living in you, He holds out to you seven precious gifts.

He will counsel you, telling you what to do when you are puzzled and disturbed. With a clear light He will pierce the fog of your confusion. Open yourself to Him. Listen to Him! Meditate on this!

He will fill you with a childlike affection so that you can approach the Divine Being with joy, making your whole life a prayer. Open yourself to Him! Receive Him! Believe this!

He will give you such strength, far beyond your own, that you will be able to undertake even "impossible" tasks without hesitation and carry them through without fear. Open yourself to Him. Trust Him! Contemplate this truth!

He will fill you with reverence for the Divine Being and you will begin to see His majesty and have complete confidence in His power. Open yourself to this reverence!

He will lead you to appreciate the "oneness" of all creation, the brotherhood of all beings, the dependence of all things on their Maker, even as He did Francis of Assisi. Open yourself to this knowledge so that everything that is may bring you closer to Me!

He will give you a deep insight into spiritual truths, disclosing their hidden meanings. You will "see" as though with new eyes, not comprehending spiritual mysteries, for this is impossible on earth, but somehow "seeing into" them. Open yourself to this understanding!

Finally, He will bring you wisdom, the most perfect of His gifts. He will light up your mind so that you will perceive the divine plan for you and for all of creation. More than this, He will fill your heart with His own love for goodness and truth. Open yourself to Him. All this is yours if only you believe.

You have My word for it: This Person, Who is the Love of My Father and Me, is My Gift to you. This Spirit, almighty, all-wise, all-good, Whom Augustine called the "bliss, the happiness, the beatitude in the Trinity, the delight of the Begetter and the Begotten," this Spirit *lives* in you.

Ask Him to make Himself known to you, revealing Himself to you through faith, so that His presence may be "real."

Ask and you will receive Him.

Seek and you will find Him.

Knock and He will not only open to you the door of divine love—He will truly dwell in you.

THE INDWELLING TRINITY

"Are you not aware that
you are the temple of God?..."
(1 Cor. 3:16).

Do you wonder, My other self, how I can "send" the Holy Spirit to live in you when God is everywhere.

Again, I am using human terms to describe the inexpressible. When I say I send the Spirit to you, I speak of a change in the relationship between Him and you. The change, of course, is in you.

When He is "sent," He "touches" you in such a way that you have a new contact with Him. He transforms you, enlightens you, enkindles in you a spark of the divine love of which He Himself is the eternal Expression.

You become a new person; you have a new life.

Moreover, He does not produce this change in you by Himself alone. All of the Divine Being's external works are performed by the Three Persons acting as the one Divine Unity.

Though you call the Father "Creator," and call Me "Wisdom," and call the Holy Spirit "Love," We are all Creator; We are all Wisdom; We are all Love. All of the divine attributes are common to and equal in the Three Persons.

The universe is not the work of the Father Person alone, but of the Tri-une God.

I taught My disciples to pray, "Our Father," but it is not only the First Person of the Trinity Who is your Father, but the Tri-une God.

I told My disciples that I would send them the Paraclete, the Consoler, but the Paraclete does not come alone. Through Him and with Him, My Father and I also come to you. Since We Three are One, where One is, there all must be; for We exist, as I have told you, only in and through One Another.

As the Father and I give ourselves to each other through the Holy Spirit, so through the same Spirit We give ourselves to you. And since We have instilled in you our own Spirit of Love, the very same Spirit which unites Us, you also are united to Us in a glorious union which you can now experience only through faith.

My Spirit belongs to you and is yours. In a deeper sense, however, you belong to Him and are His. You are His temple, His home. You are consecrated to Him and He takes possession of you.

But again, He does not, and cannot, take possession of you for Himself alone, but for the Father and Me also; so that We belong to you, yes; but you in a deeper sense belong to Us.

You are taken up into a wonderful intimacy, a common life, so to speak, with the Trinity.

This is truth. It is fact. It is reality. The presence of the Divine Being in you is real and true.

— — — —

If the external works of the Divine Being are performed by all Three Persons as One, why, you may ask, are certain powers attributed to one Person in a special manner?

Because it is good for you to think of the Three Persons in this way.

You call Us "Creator," and "Wisdom," and "Love," and thus the Trinity becomes more familiar, more personal, more intimate to you.

To stress the great Reality of the Three Persons, I spoke in this manner to My disciples. I wanted them, and you also, to be acutely conscious of this Ultimate Reality.

If I choose to adapt My explanation of supernatural truth to your capacity to comprehend, is not this what you do in your own explanation of natural truth?

Have you ever said: 'My mother gave me my life?"

But, of course, she did not. Your God gave you life, using your mother and your father as His instruments and cooperators.

Have you ever said: "My father is a good provider?"

The truth is, if you think about it, that the "providing" is done by both father and mother. Even when the father is the only wage earner, the mother in many instances decides where and how the earnings can be most effectively used. Both, then, are "providers."

Yet it is entirely appropriate for you to attribute to your mother in a special way your gift of life and to attribute to your father in a special way the role of provider.

— — — —

In only one external action can it be said that one Person of the Trinity acted alone: That is, in the Incarnation. Only the Second Person of the Trinity took to Himself a human nature and united it to the divinity in His own Person.

Not the Father, not the Holy Spirit, but I alone am the God-man. Since however, I am by My divine Nature one with the Father and the Spirit, humanity in My Person is introduced into the Trinity Itself.

This is the deepest significance of the Incarnation, of God-made-man, which we will soon begin to consider.

DELIGHT IN YOUR GOD

*"Look to him that you
may be radiant with joy"*
(Ps. 34:6).

Knowing what you now do of the Trinity, how are you to respond to the presence of the Eternal and Almighty God dwelling in you?

Surely, My other self, you already know the answer. You are to respond with immense joy and with deep and abiding love.

Rejoice in the Almighty One, for He is not only your Maker, your God Who exists before and above and outside of you—no, because of His limitless love He is *in* you, He makes Himself *belong* to you, He is *yours.*

Take joy in knowing that He is yours as your Father and you are His as His child.

Be joyful in the truth that My Love—My Spirit—the Person of Love—lives in you. He is yours and you are His.

Delight in the realization that through that Spirit you are

one with Me, joined to Me as My other self.

Many saints have tried to express the wonder of this reality.

Bernard said: "Let the soul which perceives that it has the same Spirit possessed by the Son be convinced that it is loved with fatherly affection. Have confidence, O soul, have confidence...For if carnal marriage joins two in one flesh, shall not spiritual union much more join two in one Spirit?"

Ambrose wrote: "The soul adheres to God the Word by a kiss by which the Spirit of Him Who kisses is transferred to the soul. They who kiss are not satisfied with a mere brushing of the lips, but seem to pour their very spirits into each other ... The soul craves a kiss; God the Word pours Himself wholly into that soul."

Paul said: "God has sent forth into our hearts the spirit of his Son which cries out 'Abba!' ('Father!')" (Gal. 4:6).

Words, however, can only hint at the truth. Let Me say simply that through the indwelling Trinity you are raised to a dignity, a position, and a power far above your wildest dreams.

Therefore, rejoice and love and join with Catherine of Sienna in her paean of praise.

"O all powerful and eternal Trinity! Sweet and ineffable charity, who would not be inflamed by so much love? What heart would refuse expending all for you?

"Abyss of charity! You are so intensely attached to your creatures that it would almost seem You cannot live without them! Yet You are God, having no need of us.

"What is it that inspires You with such compassion? It is love. For You have no obligation toward us, no need for us.

"What draws You then, infinite God, to me, Your puny creature? It is nothing else than Yourself, Fire of Love! Love always, Love alone has impelled and still impels your tenderness toward Your creatures, filling them with infinite graces and priceless gifts.

"Supreme Benevolence, You alone are supremely good...

"Eternal Magnificence! Immensity of Goodness! ... On whichever side I turn, I find only the abyss and fire of Your charity."

— — — —

But is this all? Do I give you My Love so that you may hoard

It and enjoy It for yourself alone?

Of course not. You are to love the indwelling Trinity with your whole heart and soul and mind and strength. But you are also to love your neighbor—not just as you love yourself but more—as *I* have loved *you*.

Having Love within you, you must express It in your acts, your words, your entire life. Oh, My other self, let the Love that is in you come forth in good works, for good works are love in action.

It is through you that the Spirit of Love Who lives in you makes Himself known in the world. Of all creatures who except man can express Love on earth?

Therefore, imitate the Spirit Who expresses the love of My Father and Me in the Trinity. Permit Him to go forth from you, and through you to recreate and renew the face of the earth.

Unless you do this, you stifle His action within you.

Even as My Father and I love each other, so also the divinity in you loves the divinity in your brother. Yes, even as our love is expressed and interchanged in the Trinity, so we wish the extension of our Love, dwelling in you, to be expressed and interchanged between you and your fellowmen.

To love in this way—which is to love as a Christian—is not easy. Even to love those who are beautiful, charming, and kind can sometimes be difficult. But to love those who are ugly, bad-tempered, foul-smelling, those you fear, those who stand in your way and strike out at you, this is more than human nature alone can do. And this is why I give you the Holy Spirit. Without Him you cannot love as a Christian. But with Him, you can; indeed you *must*.

Heed My Spirit! Do what He inspires you to do!

Be kind; be patient; be generous; be cheerful; be self-sacrificing; be magnanimous; in short, be loving!

Be so loving, indeed, that everyone you touch will be ignited by the Flame of Love living in you and will also glow and grow in that same love.

Go forth, My other Self, full of confidence! Go into the world as did the Apostles at Pentecost. You, too, are filled with the Holy Spirit. Go, remembering that the living God—*your* God—dwells in you!

V / GOD-MADE-MAN

A CLOSER UNION

*"In him everything in heaven and on earth was
created, . . . all were created
through him, and for him"* (Col. 1:16).

Because of the Trinity, the universe exists.
Because of the Trinity, humanity exists.
Because of the Trinity, I Whom you call the Christ exist as
GOD MADE MAN.

— — — —

Just as the inner activity of man overflows into outward expression as buildings, books, gardens, cars, space vehicles, so also the interior knowing and loving of the Divine Being pour themselves out exteriorly.

Therefore, *the material world exists.*

But this was not enough. Speaking somewhat poetically, you might say that because My Father has a divine Son Whom He loves with a limitless love and in Whom He takes limitless pleasure, He desired to create outside Himself other sons and daughters made to the image and likeness of that Son.

Therefore, man exists—you exist.

Again, it was too little. Could the Tri-une God, being God, stop short of the infinite?

What a poor, imperfect reflection of the internal glory of the Godhead are man and the universe. Moved, no, almost "forced" by love, the Divine One-ness longed to communicate His entire nature outside Himself not in a faint replica, but wholly, completely, in all its limitless grandeur.

For this, neither the universe nor man could suffice; only the infinite would do.

And the Word became Flesh!

From your own experience you know that it is the nature of love not only to wish to give, but to wish also to receive, and in equal measure.

"I love you with all of me," the lover exclaims and is satisfied only when his beloved responds, "And I love *you* with all of *me*."

Moreover, love desires not only equality in the intensity and completeness of the exchange, but also an equality of person.

The Divine Being, longing to communicate His goodness and love outside Himself in limitless measure, also longed to receive from outside Himself limitless love and goodness— and from an Equal.

In only one way could this be accomplished: If a created nature were joined to the divine nature in so close a union that the two would be one being, one person. Then, indeed, the Divine Being could communicate outside Himself a limitless love, and receive from outside Himself an identical love—from an Equal.

Uniting the divine and human in one Person, the Word, the Son and Second Person of the Trinity, equal to the Father and of one Being with Him, Son of God and son of man, manifests fully and perfectly the divine goodness in the created universe. He receives not just some part of His Father's love but the full measure of it; and He returns not just an imperfect imitation but an equal love.

For this reason GOD BECAME MAN.

You are not accustomed to think of the Incarnation in this way. You regard it as the price of your redemption. Indeed, My other self, I did become man for you, and My love is such that I would have done so for you alone.

But this was neither My only purpose, nor My highest purpose in becoming incarnate.

— — — —

Still why become *man*? Could I not give love and honor to My Father more fittingly through some other created nature, one higher than man's, that of an angelic spirit, for example?

No. The Ultimate Wisdom decreed that the Word should assume a created nature to show you the extent and depth of the divine love in ways that you could readily see and understand. But it was My Father's desire that *all* of creation, material and spiritual, should join in this outward communication of His goodness, and join also, to the full extent of their ability, in receiving and returning His love.

Because man is body and spirit united to form one person, he can represent both the material and the spiritual universe. Thus the Son of God, becoming the son of man, represents the whole of creation both in manifesting My Father's goodness and, in the name of all creatures, returning to Him limitless honor and love.

— — — —

Seen in this light, the Incarnation is a natural, even an inevitable, expression of the divine love. Further it is the source of a new and wonderful order embracing the totality of creation.

Spiritual beings, man, animals, plants, galaxies, solar systems, stars; all are joined together as one great manifestation of the divine goodness, power, majesty, and love. Becoming man and being, in Paul's words, "the first born" of all creation, I am in truth the Head not only of mankind but of all created beings and things.

Let this knowledge inspire you, My other self, with a new reverence for all that exists, even the ant and the atom.

Now you perceive my meaning in saying that whatever *is* would lead you to me; that every tree, bush, lake, river, pebble, and grain of sand would speak to you of the God Who made them. All of creation is a great unity, and you in your humanity and I in My humanity are part of it. In Me everything that exists pays homage to the Father. I offer it to Him. You also are privileged to offer it to Him, through Me.

When you begin to feel your own personal one-ness with the whole of creation, My other self, you can make your own the beautiful, simple, naive, yet profoundly wise prayer of Francis of Assisi:

"Be praised, my Lord, in all Your creatures,
And most of all for Monsignor Brother Sun
Who makes the day for us, and the light,
Fair is he, and radiant, and very splendid:
A semblance, Lord most high, of You.

"Be praised, my Lord, for Sister Moon and all the stars.
In heaven You have made them precious, bright and fair.

"Be praised, my Lord, for Brother Wind
and for air and clouds and every weather
By which You give sustenance to all Your creatures.

"Be praised, my Lord, for Sister Water,
Useful, humble, precious and chaste.

"Be praised, my Lord, for Brother Fire
By whom You light up the night.
Beautiful is he, and joyous, robust and strong.

"Be praised, my Lord, for our mother, Sister Earth,
Who supports and keeps us, and produces for us
Her varied fruits and colored flowers and grass.

"Oh, praise and bless my Lord, and thankful be
And serve Him all with great humility."

YOU ARE OF GOD'S FAMILY

*"...a child is born to us,
a son is given us..."*
(Is. 9:5).

One member of the human race not only has God dwelling in Him, but is Himself God.

This holds special meaning for you.

It means that when you are joined to Me you *belong to My Father's own intimate family.*

Of your own nature you are simply My Father's creature. But since He wanted you and all men to be more, He implanted in man a super-human life, a wonderful communication of and participation in His own divine life, which you call "grace." By grace you become not merely My Father's creature but His friend and even His adopted child.

Man lost this gift of grace, thus breaking the line of communication between the Divine Being and himself. Yet, through the incalculable measure of the Divine Being's love, this loss provided the occasion for the incomparably greater gift that would flow from My Incarnation.

Whereas before, mankind carried in it only an offshoot of the divine life, now as the result of God-made-man, one Man, one Member of your race, *is* God.

In this singular Man a human nature does not exist by itself. No, for just this once, a distinct human nature is incorporated into a divine Person, so that the Son of God, the Second Person of the Trinity, possessor of the divine nature, becomes also through his possession of a human nature the son of man.

Somewhat as skin can be engrafted on your body so that it becomes one with and part of your body, so, in a sense, a human nature was instantaneously "engrafted" onto My divine nature, causing the divine and the human to be joined in one Person.

Mark well the phrase, "in *one* Person;" that is the essence of God-Made-Man.

It means that the Son of Man is not merely a man in whom the nature of God is also somehow present. *He is God made flesh.*

Rather than being a friend or an adopted human son of the Divine Being by decree or by gift—which was all that any man previously could be—I, the Christ, am the Father's *natural* Son, His Son by inalienable right, His divine Son living in the created universe.

With the Incarnation the *fullness* of the divine life *belongs* to one member of the human race.

— — — —

But, how does this place you in a new relationship to God? How does it make you a member of God's family?

As My Father's Son, I am one with Him and the Holy Spirit. As Mary's Son, however, I am a member with you of the human family. Somewhat as two families are united through intermarriage, the union of My divinity with My humanity unites all members of the human race with the Divine Being.

When the king is your monarch and you are simply his subject, that is one relationship. But when the king marries into your family, and his love produces a son, you and all members of your family are joined in a new relationship to the king himself.

Somewhat similarly, through My Incarnation, the family of man becomes the family of God.

The entire race, indeed, is lifted up to a kind of one-ness with the ONE WHO IS—because *humanity is introduced into the Trinity; a man is placed on God's throne.*

This, indeed, is a mind-shattering truth. The full consequences for mankind are incomprehensible. Only by reflecting on it at great length can you begin to grasp the inconceivable dignity to which the Incarnation has elevated the human race.

Listen, My other self, to what some of My saints have said as they tried to express the meaning of God-made-man.

Listen to Augustine: "God has become man that man might become God."

To Cyprian: "What man is Christ wished to be, that man in turn might be what Christ is."

To Irenaeus: "He became what we are, in order that He might make us what He is."

To Leo: "He so united Himself to us and us to Him, that the descent of God to the human level was at the same time the ascent of man to the divine level."

To Athanasius: "As the Lord became man by putting on our body, so shall we men be deified, assumed by His flesh."

Contemplate these truths, My other self: Contemplate and begin to know yourself!

YOU ARE GOD'S SON

*"You are no longer a slave but
a son! And the fact that you
are a son makes you an heir,
by God's design"* (Gal 4:7).

You do not yet appreciate, My other self, how intimate a member of the divine family you are. Your relationship to the Divine Being is not merely that of an in-law, a relative by marriage. It is far more.

When the Son of God in the Trinity became also the son of man in Mary's womb, I made it possible for all men to be My Father's *sons*, My Father's *daughters*.

This is why I tell you to pray: "Our Father."

Never before My incarnation was any man able to address the Divine Being with full truth, as "Father." Now you not only can; you should; you must.

Think, My other self, what it must mean to have *God* for your Father.

You sometimes say that a child has his father or his mother in him; and he does indeed, for he has taken his body, his faculties, his nervous system, his talents from theirs.

Ah, but there is a great deal more of your Heavenly Father in you than there is of your human parents.

Although your human father cooperated in giving you natural life, he himself is not actually present in you. But your heavenly Father, in a mysterious but real way, is present in you and dwells in you.

Your human father has sometimes looked at you and seen reflected his own features, his own mannerisms. Because of the Incarnation, when the eternal Father looks at you He sees Himself in you—because He sees Me in you, His eternal Son who perfectly reflects him.

And He loves you.

Because I have made Him your Father it makes sense for Me to say to you, "Be not solicitous about your life."

Because He is truly your Father, He must protect you and provide for you.

How wonderful it is to have the Almighty One for your Father; to be His son or daughter. Do you recall what I said in our first conversation—that My gift would free you from worry and fear? What have you to dread, you who are your Father's child?

What have you to fear from insults or barbed words, from loss of prestige or human respect, from scoffing or ridicule; what have you who have such a Father to fear from danger to your dear ones, from perils to your health or possessions, even from death itself?

Trust Him! He has given you the right to demand from Him all the privileges of a son or daughter, far more than a prince or princess could dare ask of a human king. You are heir to His kingdom.

He may test you, as a king might test his child, but He cannot fail you. Never!

He delights in a certain boldness of love on your part. Do not be reserved toward Him but outgoing. *Act* like God's son. *Act* like God's daughter. Have the confidence a son or daughter of the Divine Being—HE WHO IS—should have. Act as a prince or princess, whose trust is unbounded, whose love has no horizon.

Place yourself in His care and He will give you everything good. Knowing all your needs, He will often satisfy them even before you ask, because He is your Father. But sometimes He will wait for your request, because this, too, is good for you.

Call on Him for anything and He is obligated by His Father's love to grant it. Or if it is not good for you and He says, "No," then He must give you what is better.

For what will you ask? Peace in the world? An end to violence? Good health for your dear ones? Holiness for yourself and those you love most dearly?

Make all these requests if you wish. But there will come a time when suddenly you will understand that really you want to ask for nothing—except that your Father's will be done.

If you love Him as a son or a daughter—and you do—then

what you want above all is the fulfillment of His will.

If you trust Him—and you do—then the best you can do is to throw everything into His arms and let Him dispose of it as His wisdom determines.

If you have faith in Him—and you have—then you will not want to "play God." You will want Him to decide what shall be.

Suddenly you will understand that since He has given men freedom to choose, it is His plan that men should use their freedom. You will remember that He Himself prized human freedom so highly that He sent Me to persuade men to goodness but did not stifle their freedom even when men used it to crucify Me. Are you, then, to ask Him to coerce the will of those who rebel?

You cannot. All you can say is, "Father, your kingdom come. Your will be done." And this is the best prayer of all, the prayer of Gethsemane, the prayer of Calvary.

This is how you will change the world and renew Christianity. This is how you will be another Paul—another Christ—in truth, My other self.

Through the Holy Spirit, He will make clear to you what you are to do, and you have only to follow His directions.

— — — —

Now again I must ask whether you see a new significance in your relationship to your fellowmen. Do you understand that all men, the entire family of whatever race, color, nation, or station in life, are sons and daughters of My Father; are all joined to Me and to you through Me?

True, the union of each individual with Me becomes a living union only through faith. Yet the entire race of man in a mystical but real way forms one person with Me. For this reason, what you do to even the least of your brothers and sisters, white, brown, or black, friend or enemy, kind or cruel, pleasant to be with or humanly repulsive; this you do also to Me.

You are the King's son, the King's daughter. So are they,

even the lowliest of them. Be kind, be generous, be magnanimous, therefore, as a prince or princess ought to be to other members of the royal family.

How blessed you are in knowing who you are when so many seek their identity. Teach them. Are they to go through their whole lives never realizing their dignity and destiny? Help them, that they, too, may understand what it means to be My Father's child. Teach them, that they also may be fearless, kind, generous, magnanimous as all My Father's children should be.

This is the task of a prince of the kingdom. This is the role of the King's son.

I HAVE MADE MY FATHER YOUR DEBTOR

"...he emptied himself...
being born in the likeness
of men" (Phil. 2:7).

Because you are His son, your heavenly Father will refuse you nothing that is for your good.

But even if He could refuse as a Father, justice makes it impossible for Him to deny you.

The awe-ful fact is that He is your Debtor.

"The Eternal God in debt to me?" you exclaim, "Impossible!"

No, it is true. My Father, the Almighty One, HE WHO IS, actually is in your debt. The price of love and service I paid Him in your name is infinite; therefore, He no longer bestows His choicest blessings on you out of sheer generosity. Now He gives them to you as your right and your due. He owes you His aid. He is your Debtor.

Simply by taking a human nature and combining it with the divinity—a mystery, I repeat, but an actuality—I earned for you a vast treasury of supernatural rights and gifts such as no created being could ever earn for itself.

And by taking a human nature in its condition of *lowliness,* I gained for you even more.

The Word could have given His humanity every possible good; He could have appeared on earth in a body transfigured and glorified such as when I rose from the tomb.

Instead, I chose, as Paul puts it, to "empty" Myself and become as truly human as you.

You find it difficult, My other self, to think of Me as both fully divine and fully human. You regard My humanity as different from yours, far above it, free from the weaknesses you see in your own nature.

It is not so. Let My mother tell you; she knows what I did; she saw how I lived. Listen to her.

From conception until death, like any other human being, my son, Jesus, obeyed the laws of growth. In my womb He was as helpless as you were in your mother. Like you, His eyes opened, His heart developed its rhythmic lifelong beat, He learned to flex His fingers and to move His head and arms and legs. I felt Him stir within me, even as your mother felt you.

After He was born in Bethlehem, He fed instinctively at my breast. When I placed Him in the manger He lay in the typical baby position, head turned to one side, one arm extended in that direction, the other bent, with His hand resting on His little chest.

Like any Jewish infant boy He was circumcised. Like any baby, He suffered from heat and cold and discomfort. And like any mother, I soothed and conforted Him. As He grew, His eyes followed me as I moved about. He began to reach out for things. After a while He was able to sit up; to hold and poke and pluck at objects with His fingers; to creep, to stand and walk; and finally to run and jump.

He began to speak words, then phrases, then sentences. I recall how He built little towers by piling one object on another, how He learned to scribble, to use a spoon and feed Himself a little, to put on His clothes. He grew taller and His teeth came in;

He learned to string beads, draw crude pictures, hammer a nail, saw a piece of wood.

Like any toddler He fell sometimes, and like any small boy skinned His knees and elbows; and when I cleaned out the dirt it hurt Him even as when your mother did it to you.

At My knee, He learned to recite the morning and evening prayers of devout Jews: "Hear, O Israel, the Lord our God is one Lord." And the psalms and blessings: "Blessed art thou, Lord God, who bringeth forth the bread from the earth." "Blessed art thou, Lord God, who created the fruit of the vine." "Blessed be He who gave the law."

He liked to go off on walks with Joseph and to play the vigorous games that boys enjoy. He grew not only in body and strength, but in mind and knowledge. I know this is true. He was, and is, my Son—and He was, and is, fully human.

— — — —

Precisely how the infinite Word could grow in knowledge is a mystery and will remain so. Again, however, analogies may open the door a little.

First, you must understand that My humanity has no existence apart from My divinity. I am not a man to whom divinity has been added, but the eternal Word to Whom humanity has been added; not man become God, but God become man; not a human person, but a divine Person with two natures, one of them human.

As the Son of God, all knowledge is Mine. But as the son of man possessing a truly human nature—a body, mind, and spirit—this aspect of My Person could, and did, develop in human ways; in human knowledge, in human psychology; in human emotion, as well as in human strength.

You understand that divine power is different from human strength not only in degree but in kind. So also divine knowledge is different in kind from human knowledge. Further, just as the divinity is not apprehensible to human intelligence, so the divine knowing is not apprehensible to human knowing. You cannot begin to understand how the divine "intelligence" encompasses all truth.

But surely you recognize that the Son of God, as God, has no more need for human knowledge than He has for human strength. Just as the might of the All-mighty may be said to encompass human might without possessing it, so also the infinite knowing of the Son of God encompasses human finite knowing without possessing it.

To the Son of God in the Trinity all truth is known perfectly, unchangeably, NOW. This does not mean, however, that the human intelligence of GOD-MADE-MAN could not advance in human knowledge or learn to do in human ways what the Son of God has no need to do.

As the Word, I know perfectly all the truths that the Scriptures impart to man imperfectly; but to know these truths in My human intelligence as man knows them, I learned to read the Scriptures.

Because I came to show humanity how God would live if He were man, I truly lived as man.

Accepting humanity in all its weaknesses, I grew in body, in muscle and stamina, in speech and thought and reason.

So doing, I gave you a Model to follow. And I made My eternal Father your Debtor.

THE TOTAL SACRIFICE

"In his own body he brought your sins
to the cross... By his wounds you
were healed" (1 Peter 4:24).

It was the totality of My sacrifice as the son of man that placed the Eternal Father in your debt. To understand this, My other self, you must see suffering as it really is.

My death on the cross, as Paul said, was a stumbling block to the Jews and an absurdity to the Gentiles. But the wisdom of God is the foolishness of men—because men know so little about love.

To man, suffering and death are debasing; they are evils to be dreaded. Actually, to suffer, even to die, far from being of itself debasing, can be ennobling. What nobler love is possible for a man than willingly to lay down his life for another?

If out of regard for My Father, and you, I endured sufferings such as no other man ever could, it was to give both Him and you the most extravagant proof of My love.

A drop of the blood I shed in being circumcised or that oozed from My knees and elbows when I fell as a boy, a single tear from My eyes, one bead of perspiration as a result of My labor, one stab of pain as I hit My thumb with the hammer at Joseph's bench—any of these offered in the name of humanity would have been more than enough to restore men to My Father's friendship.

But because I wished to manifest My love to the highest degree possible for a created nature I permitted suffering to overcome Me even unto death.

Never think of My Passion as something that "happened" to Me—something to which I merely acceded because it was My Father's will.

Had I Myself not willed it, pain and death could never have touched Me.

I laid down My life; no one took it from Me.

To give My Father the ultimate in self-surrender, self-sacrifice, and love through an extreme self-annihilation; this was My highest goal in assuming human frailties.

And because I offered the ultimate in self-surrender, self-sacrifice, and love not in My Name alone but in yours, you whom I have joined to Me in the oneness of the human family, My Father is now your Debtor and He can refuse you nothing. Henceforth, whatever you ask of Him in My name, *He must give you.*

This indeed is what I plainly told My disciples.

As Chrysostom said, you did not receive only so much grace as was needed to do away with sin, but so much more that you are regenerated, redeemed, and sanctified, made brother of the Only-begotten One and a co-heir with Me to My Father's kingdom.

It was not My Father's plan that I should simply bring down to men from heaven this "one-ness" with Me. No, I had actually to earn it, to buy it, and thus in a real sense to obligate My Father to establish it.

Receiving from a woman the flesh and blood I offered, I became the representative of the entire race of men.

My whole mortal life culminating in Calvary, then, is the purchase money which makes My Father your Debtor. By accepting My sacrifice, He bound Himself to give you every blessing; specifically, the right to be the temple of the Holy Spirit; the right to be His true and real offspring; the right after your death to have body and soul reunited in glory; the right, finally, to see the Persons of the Trinity face to face and to be united with them in an existence of perfect peace and perfect goodness, which is the fulness of joy, a sharing in the glory of God Himself.

— — — —

This is what My becoming man means to you; by it the human race is changed into a divine race.

By it, you receive sonship with Me and become heir with Me to My heavenly throne, so that where I am you may eventually be.

By it, all that I did as man, you do also simply by uniting your will with Mine; and what you do, I do too, provided only that you do it in My Name.

By it, I live in you, speak in you, experience suffering and joy in you, am clothed, sheltered and fed in you; for I am one with you.

By it, you are given a new vision of what you are called to be—a noble being, free from meanness and bitterness; a loving being, devoid of even one iota of hate; a serene being, fully confident of your destiny; an unselfish being, recognizing that you need seek nothing for yourself because your Father Himself has care of you.

By it, the divine knowledge and love are projected and continued outside of the Trinity in all their limitless grandeur— and creation in its entirety is united, raised up, and given power to glorify the living God in an infinite way.

This is the meaning of God-made-man.

VI / GOD IN THE EUCHARIST

THE GREATEST LOVE

*"With age-old love
I have loved you..."* Jer. 31:3).

You might think, My other self, that no more could possibly be done to communicate the divine life and to love and serve My Father in the created world than was accomplished by the Son of God's becoming the son of man and thus uniting the whole of creation in manifesting My Father's glory.

Again, you would be thinking in limited terms.

If you knew the divine nature, you would understand that more had to be done.

The Divine Being, I have told you, expresses His love and knowledge perfectly within Himself through the Trinity. And He expresses them perfectly outside Himself through Me, the Christ, **GOD—MADE—MAN.**

Since what I returned to the Father in love and service was done in the name of the whole race of men, humanity was enabled to love and serve Him in a manner far above human power.

But still the Divine Being—being love without limit—willed to do more. This return of love and service offered in the name of the whole race of man, encompassing as it was, was still not the most perfect return possible for *you*. Only if you individually were joined to Me *directly* would this perfect return become possible for you as an individual.

But how could you be?

Could it not be accomplished in something of the way I became man? Not only did I live physically in My Mother's body, but in so doing I joined her to Me spiritually in a union immeasurably closer than the physical. Is there some way in which I could live physically and spiritually in you also?

The Eucharist is My answer. Through the Eucharist I can become as intimate to you as your own flesh, blood and bone, as intimate to you as your own soul.

Through it, I can join Myself directly to you; and though you fully retain your humanity, personality, and free will, now, more than ever, whatever I do you do also, and whatever you do in union with Me I do also. The Eucharist solves the problem.

— — — —

On Calvary I offered My Father a supreme sacrifice of loving self-annihilation. But love never wants to be given just once and that's the end of it. No, love longs to renew itself endlessly.

Is there some way in which I could renew My love offering through innumerable repetitions until the very end of time?

Again, the Eucharist is My answer. Through it I can continue to be really and substantially present in the world. And through it My love offering can be made not just by Me in the name of mankind but by you individually and by millions like you.

Thus the Father can receive not only from Me, but from you, perfect love, perfect service, perfect praise, perfect sacrifice.

— — — —

Further, is there some way in which I could return in glory to My Father and yet stay with you, not just as one Person among billions, but as one directly united to you and to each individual?

Yes—through the Eucharist.

— — — —

Finally, is there some way in which, here and now while you are on earth, I could give you My pledge of a future union with the Trinity, a pledge so complete and overwhelming that you could not mistake its meaning or doubt its efficacy?

Again, the Eucharist makes it possible.

— — — —

All this by human standards must seem too good to be true. But does not your very existence outrage probability?

You are the end result of an almost incredibly intricate chain of interlocking circumstances. You exist because at one precise instant in history one specific male reproductive cell out of millions of available cells fertilized a specific female cell. Had two other cells united, not you but your brother or sister would have been conceived. Your existence, therefore, depended on your unique conception at one precise instant in time. The same applies to each of your parents. Had their conceptions not occurred at the precise points they did, your parents would never have existed and could never have given birth to you. All the way back to the beginning of the human race this chain of circumstances extends. Just one interruption anywhere along the line, and *you* would not be.

But you were conceived and born and have come to this present moment; and this not because of chance, but because from all eternity your God wanted *you* to live.

And so you began as a microscopic seed united to a tiny egg. Is it not "too good to be true" that from such insignificant blobs of material the living "you" of today should have developed? Is it "logical" that from such a beginning individuals should emerge capable of composing and singing beautiful music; writing and speaking magnificent thoughts; constructing towering buildings, enormous bridges, great cities, vehicles to explore space?

Is not the universe itself too marvelously complex to be true? Is it within the realm of probability as you know it that matter should be almost entirely empty; that light should travel at such speed; that space should contain innumerable billions of stars; that distances in the universe should be so inconceivably vast; or that the universe itself should be so incredibly old?

Surely, none of this "makes sense." Measured by human

capacities it cannot possibly be. Yet it is.

You see the folly of measuring the finite universe by human standards. When will you stop cutting your God to your measure?

Why should the Eucharist be too good to be true? Why, that is, if you believe that the Son of God became the son of man?

If the Son of God did not disdain to accept humanity in its lowliness, why should the son of man hesitate to perpetuate His life among men and give Himself to you individually through this means?

You must not regard My mortal life as a kind of historical interlude; as though in the beginning I was God; then for a time I lived on earth as man; but when this period was over I went back to being God again. Do you think that once I ascended to My Father I was still interested in the world as God, but no longer as man?

I did not become man for some 30 years and then cease to be human. I am no less human now than I was when I walked in Palestine; no less concerned about the world now *as man* than I was then; no less conscious of it *as man*, no less involved in it *as man*, no less aware of and interested in the progress of mankind *as man*. The fact of the Eucharist alone should convince you of this; the fact that in the Eucharist I am still with you not only spiritually, but *physically* also, as the God-Man.

Could you but begin to understand the goodness, the love, and the power of the divinity; could you but glimpse as from afar the meaning of goodness without limit, of love without limit, of power without limit; could you achieve but one iota of appreciation of My yearning that all mankind should unite in loving and serving My Father and that all creation should be one in manifesting His goodness; then you would see that My becoming man and My inventing the Eucharist are both not only harmonious with the nature of the divinity but are actually to be expected of it.

Indeed, could you have conceived of these possibilities before they occurred, and fathomed however faintly the limitless nature of divine love, you would have known with certainty that the Incarnation and the Eucharist *must* happen.

As My love drove Me to the Incarnation so that I could be one with the human race, so that same love drove Me to the Eucharist so that I could be "one" with you.

God-made-man is wholly logical—and the Eucharist is inevitable—because infinite love would have it no other way.

THE BREAD OF LIFE

*"Taste and see
how good the Lord is"*
(Ps. 34:9).

The multitude sought Me after they had been fed with the loaves and fishes, and I began to tell them about the new Food, the new Bread, I would give them which would bring life to the whole world.

"I Myself am the bread of life." I said to them; "No one who comes to Me shall ever be hungry, no one who believes in Me shall ever thirst."

As well they might, they wondered what I meant.

I repeated and elaborated. "I am the bread of life. I Myself am the living bread come down from heaven. If anyone eats this bread, he shall live forever; the bread I will give is My flesh, for the life of the world."

They began to argue with one another, asking how I could give My flesh to be eaten, and protesting that this could not be.

So I said further: "If you do not eat the flesh of the Son of Man and drink His blood, you have no life in you. He who feeds on My flesh and drinks My blood has life eternal, and I will raise him up on the last day. For My flesh is real food, and My blood real drink. The man who feeds on My flesh and drinks My blood remains in Me and I in him."

And finally: "Just as ... I have life because of the Father, so the man who feeds on Me will have life because of Me. This is the bread that came down from heaven...the man who feeds on this bread shall live forever" (John 6:35, 48, 51, 53-54, 56-58).

At this, many turned away. "Impossible," they muttered. They thought I meant them to eat My body in the form in which they saw Me standing before them. They were not cannibals. They walked off.

Others, however, having faith that I knew what I was doing, that somehow it would come out right, stayed. When I asked, "Do you want to leave Me too?" Peter answered for them.

"Lord, to whom shall we go? You have the words of eternal life."

This is what I wanted from them, this faith. It is what I want from you.

At the Last Supper their belief was rewarded. Then they discovered that it did indeed come out right. They ate and drank as I directed them; they received the life-giving bread that I had promised them; and there was nothing carnal, nothing cannibalistic, about it.

— — — —

What precisely is the Eucharist which makes the "impossible" easy? What took place at the Last Supper when I said, "This is My body. This is My blood?" What occurs when the priest repeats these words in the Mass?

Essentially this. The body of the son of man, glorified and incorruptible as it was when it came from the tomb, becomes present under the appearances of bread and wine. Bread and wine are no longer there; My body and blood *are* there. And there they remain so long as the appearances of bread and wine endure.

These are the essentials. But there is much more about the Eucharist that you should know.

How is it accomplished?

Surely, this is not incomprehensible. When you eat bread and wine, are not these changed into *your* body and blood; not instantly it is true, but nonetheless are they not so changed by laws that the Divine Being has ordained?

Why should He not perform in an instant what normally He chooses to perform in a matter of hours?

But how can this wafer be a body? It is so small. Where are its arms, its legs; where is its flesh?

You are thinking in human terms again, just as did the disbelieving ones centuries ago. Even though I told them that the "living bread" was not like the bread their ancestors ate as manna in the desert, they could not accept the truth. This seeming morsel of bread is indeed My body, whole and entire. But this does not mean that My body is confined by or limited to the physical dimensions of the Host.

Stop limiting Me, My other self!

Realize that the living bread of the Eucharist is predominantly spiritual. It is not the mortal body of the Christ Who walked the roads of Palestine before the resurrection. No, it is My glorified body—immortal, incorruptible.

It is the property of a glorified body to be capable of appearing under different guises. This happened at the Transfiguration on the mountain when Peter, James, and John saw My face shining like the sun and My garments dazzled them with a whiteness beyond anything of earth. It occurred again after the Resurrection when Mary of Magdala did not recognize Me near the tomb. It took place still another time when the disciples on the road to Emmaus did not know Me; and yet again when seven of the Apostles, even including Peter and John, did not recognize Me at Lake Tiberius.

Until I revealed Myself, none of these knew Me in the state of glorification.

If now I choose to disguise My glorified body under the appearance of bread, who is to say I cannot?

— — — —

But let Me tell you more about the Eucharist.

It is the Holy Spirit Who does for Me in the Eucharist something similar to what He did twice before: in Nazareth and in the tomb.

In Nazareth the Spirit took Mary's mortal flesh and blood, long nourished by bread and wine, and changed them into My *mortal* body and blood, Now, in the Eucharist, He takes the bread and wine on the altar and changes them into My *glorified* body and blood.

To put it another way, as in Nazareth the Spirit enabled Me to become one body with Mary, now through the Eucharist He enables Me to become one body with you.

After I died and was buried in the tomb, the Holy Spirit reclaimed My inanimate corpse from death, glorified it and made it immortal. In the Eucharist He again instantaneously transforms inanimate substances into that same glorified and immortal Body. The Eucharist, in a sense, "renews" both Christmas and Easter.

In some ways, indeed, the marvel of the Eucharist exceeds even the marvel of the Resurrection. My risen Body cannot naturally reside in more than one place at a time; it could not, for example, be simultaneously in the upper room in Jerusalem and on the road to Emmaus.

In the Eucharist, however, that same Body, existing on a higher plane, physical and material but dominated by spiritual qualities, has some of the characteristics of the divinity Itself; specifically, of being present wholly and undivided in many places at once and of being invisibly present in the very core or center of things. It has the power of transfiguring you; of entering into you, giving you its own life and transforming you into Me.

I endow It with these properties of the divinity Itself so that I can dwell in you individually and in all who receive Me in the closest possible way; that you may have life and have it more abundantly.

If you ask again, how can this be? My answer is, "Why should it not be?" Is the Son of God bound by physical laws? Is He not able to be present wherever and in what manner He pleases, not by going from place to place, but by staying where He is and existing elsewhere also, just as He chooses?

When you address a roomful of people, do not all hear the

same words? If you speak over the radio or appear on television, do not your words and your image in the very same split second of time reach millions of people in thousands of separate communities? And is not the same message delivered to each person wholly and entirely?

If such power is given to natural forces to convey human words, cannot the omnipotent and coeternal Word of the Father give to the flesh and blood which He has joined to His Divine Person the power to be in many places at once?

So, you see, My other self, you have no reason to doubt Me or to shrink from the promised Eucharist. The Eucharist is your *spiritual* food. Since it is physical, it does indeed nourish your body, but not in a distasteful way. The real purpose of the Eucharist is to feed not your flesh but your soul.

It is a heavenly bread, "the bread which comes down from heaven." Incorruptible, it cannot be disfigured by any defects of the flesh. You do not, you cannot, receive it in a carnal, bloody manner.

This, then, is the Eucharist: A most intimate union of individuals, like you, with the divinity Itself. Through it I enter into you and live in you so that you, who have become of My family through My Incarnation, may now partake in the most intimate way of My very life. What feeds and nourishes you is the divine energy of the Son of God inhabiting a glorified human Body.

BE CHRIST!

"The man who feeds on my flesh
...remains in me and I in him" (John 6:57)

You understand, My other self, that when you eat ordinary bread what you eat becomes you, for that is the purpose of your eating.

But when you receive the bread of life, you are changed into Me, because that is the purpose of the Eucharist.

Like the union of a mother with the child in her womb, the Eucharistic union is a joining together of two living bodies, only more enduring and far more complete.

While the physical joining of mother and child ends with birth, My physical union with you can be renewed daily; and its effects remain even after the physical presence is no more.

While the child is "bone of its mother's bone, flesh of her flesh," the Eucharist union is more; for the Eucharist engrafts your whole being into Me. As I unite My body with you, so I unite My divinity with you.

The Eucharist Host penetrates into the very core of your being, to permeate you with My love, to engulf and encompass you in the divine life, so that you become not only one in body but truly one in spirit with Me.

I cannot say it too often: *You* are changed into *Me*.

This, of course, is contrary to your mode of thinking. You think of your receiving Me in the Eucharist, and truly yours is the action of taking the Host. But from that instant, the activity is Mine. You take the Host into your mouth, but I take you into Myself. I am your food, but in all that matters you are transformed so that you become more Me than you are yourself. Your blood in a sense becomes My blood, your flesh My flesh; but more important, your spirit partakes of and becomes united to My divinity so that your whole being, body and spirit, is transformed as is a drop of water when it is added to a cup of wine.

The earthly bread on the altar is changed into heavenly Bread; so also are you transformed from an earthly to a heavenly being.

— — — —

This introduces a new concept of the way I live in you and I want you to mark it well.

You can say that I live in you, for this is true. In a deeper sense, however, it is you who live in Me.

The ocean does indeed dwell in the drop of seawater, since the droplet is of the ocean and made up of the same elements as the ocean. More precisely, however, the drop of water dwells in the ocean.

Therefore, while it is proper for you to think of Me as dwelling in you—as you have been doing—you must now begin thinking of the Divine Presence more and more in terms of your living in your God somewhat as the drop of water lives in the sea.

Form the habit of doing this, and you will come to see more clearly your place in the divine plan and your role in the created world.

— — — —

I say to you that through the Eucharist you live in Me and I immerse you in My life.

What does this mean? Again, let us turn to analogies.

The rays of the sun cause a flower to grow and bloom. But suppose the flower were infiltrated in some way by the sun itself so that the sun dwelt in the flower or more properly the flower dwelt in the sun. It would be transformed, made, so to speak, a small sun itself from which light and heat radiate.

Or suppose that the sun by which you are warmed and in the rays of which you bask, were to unite itself with you, changing you into itself; then *you* would give out rays of heat, making all things around you warm. You would emit light, making your surroundings bright.

Through the Eucharist you are in truth not merely warmed and illuminated by My Presence. Because I am the light of the world and you are in Me and I in you, you also become the light of the world. And you must let your light shine before men so that they may see your good works and glorify the Father of all.

If you ask Me, "Lord, what must I do to let my light shine before men?" My answer is—"Be Christ!" It is for this that I make you one body, one blood, one spirit with Me; so that you should become in truth a Christ-bearer, a *you*-bearing Christ —truly My other self.

Yes, be Christ! Open yourself to My action and you will

"put on" My person. I will cause you to think My very thoughts, to desire what I desire, so that it will almost be true that your will is replaced with Mine. You will have in you what Paul called the "mind of Jesus Christ."

Paul knew well that I had transformed him into Me. When he carried the Good News to far places, he was well aware that I was continuing My work through him. When he preached and baptized and wrote and suffered persecution, he understood that I did all these things in him, using him as My instrument.

Paul knew, and because he knew he said, "I live now, not I, but Christ lives in me."

So it is to be with you. This is why I can call you My other self—because I transform you into Me.

So I say to you, when you receive Me immerse yourself in this thought:

Christ is in Me and I am in Him. Christ has changed me into Himself. I live now, not I, but I live in Christ and He lives in me. Therefore, I am Christ! *I am Christ! I AM CHRIST!"*

This is not blasphemy. You do not equate yourself with Me. I am the Eternal Word and you are only man. We are not identical. You are you and I am I. Yet in a way which you cannot understand you are identified with Me and you *are* Christ.

Unless you are Christ, you fail Me. You repudiate Me. You throw back in My face My gift to you.

Go, then! Go—and be Christ! This is the whole point of the Eucharist.

How? By thinking and acting as I did—and doing it in My Name.

By surrendering your body, your will, your whole being, to the Father as I did.

By offering Him homage, adoration, love, in union with Me.

By loving your brother as I have loved him.

By blessing him, as I blessed him in Galilee and Judea.

By smiling on him.

By being quick to help him in need; in such small things as holding open a door so he may pass before you; and in such larger ones as feeding him when he is hungry, caring for him when he is sick, sharing your wealth with him when he is poor, defending him when he is abused.

By being charitable, open-hearted, and open-handed.

By giving of yourself. By giving and giving and giving!

Let Me live on in you. Continue My work. Do today what I did yesterday.

Be Christ, My other self. BE CHRIST!

ONE BODY IN CHRIST

"...we, though many, are
one body in Christ"
(Rom. 12:5).

You have seen, My other self, that all of creation is a "one-ness."

You have become somewhat aware of the far more wonderful "one-ness" which unites God and humanity through My Incarnation.

You have caught a glimpse of the inconceivable "one-ness" with Me which is yours in the Eucharist.

Now I want you to understand a little the almost equally incomprehensible "one-ness" by which you are bound to your fellowmen through that same Eucharist.

Do you recall how I prayed to My Father on the night of the Last Supper?

"I pray...that all may be one, as You, Father, are in Me and I in you; I pray that they may be one in Us...

"I have given them the glory you gave Me, that they may be one, as We are one—I living in them, You living in Me—that their unity may be complete. So shall the world know that you sent Me" (John 17:20-23).

Note especially the words "...so shall the world know that You sent Me." This is how your fellowmen will recognize that the faith you profess is indeed from God: by your complete *one-ness* with your fellow believers; by the love which cements your relationship with them; by the way you think and speak and act concerning them.

The way of love which you follow gives evidence of My own divinity.

It is through the Eucharist that "one-ness" is perfected. The Eucharist joins you to Me; and in Me it joins you, on the one hand, with the Trinity, and on the other, with all who partake of it.

Hence Paul could write, "Many though we are, we are one body, for we all partake of the one loaf" (1 Cor: 10,17).

And John of Damascus, echoing Paul, could say: By Communion we are "united and made one with each other. For since we partake of the one bread, we are all made the one body and one blood of Christ; and inasmuch as we belong to the one body of Christ, we are also made members of one another."

— — — —

In our last conversation I urged you to tell yourself over and over, "I live in Christ and He lives in me. Therefore, in a sense, I am Christ." But if this is true of you, it must be true also of all who receive Me. They, too, are Christ.

Look at your brother. See him as one who lives in Me. You and he are *one in Me*—one body of which you are a part—one body in which we all are joined.

Yes, look at your brother who like you has received Me, and think: "I am I and you are you. But we are both in Christ and therefore we are one."

Look at the old Negro woman and reflect, "We are one. We are together in Christ, we are one in Him."

Look at the boy, the young girl, in front of you, and say to yourself, "We are one, you and I, we are one."

Look at the baby in its mother's arms—"we are one, little child."

Look at the merchant, the laborer, the farmer, the clerk, the doctor—"We are one, you with me and I with you."

Look at the priest—"We, you and I, are one in the Lord."

In the Eucharist, you receive Life, Light, and Love, but not for yourself alone.

As the blessings given to Me in My human nature were intended also to be extended to you, were indeed given to you so that through Me you could become a son of God, so your blessings must be shared.

Because of one-ness, the kindness you extend to your brother you extend also to Me, and through Me to yourself.

Therefore, when you go to your brother's aid in his sickness, homelessness, loneliness, or discouragement, you come to My aid also. Look at him and see Me in him.

When you visit your brother in prison, or comfort him in grief, you visit and comfort Me. Look at him and see Me.

When you help your brother in his work, or treat him to lunch, you help and treat Me. Look at him and see Me.

When he thanks you for treating or helping, or visiting, or comforting him, I thank you also. Look into his grateful eyes and see Mine.

Listen to his words and hear My voice.

Feel the touch of his hand and know that it is My hand, too, that touches you.

But what if you frown rather than smile, reject rather than give, hate rather than love?

Then it must follow that—terrible thought!—because of one-ness again, the kindness you withhold from your brother, you withhold from Me—and from yourself.

— — — —

Reflect, and you will begin to understand how I could say to Paul, "Saul, Saul, why do you persecute Me?"

Reflect, and you will see why it is that I will say to you on the last day: "I was hungry and you gave Me food." And why it is that if you should ask Me, "Lord, when did I see You hungry and feed you?" My answer must be:

"WHATEVER YOU DID TO THE LEAST OF THESE YOU DID TO ME—BECAUSE YOU AND THEY ARE ONE IN ME"

THE COMPLETE UNION

*"How shall I make a return
to the Lord for all the good
he has done for me?"* (Ps. 115:12).

Are you thinking, My other self, "Lord, these wonderful truths you have told me—I believe them on your word. But I have so little consciousness of this. Should I not feel it much more?"

No. As I told you, what is spiritual cannot be felt, unless I wish it to be. The wonder of the Eucharist can be known to you only by faith.

On the other hand, you are quite right to ask why, if the Eucharist floods you with divine life, its apparent results in you are so weak.

If the results are disappointing, it is only because your desire, selflessness, and love are weak. These are the valves which determine the effect of My presence on you. You can open wide the valves to let the divine life flood into you or shut them off so that you receive only a trickle. The choice is yours.

The way to open yourself fully to My presence is by willing with a great yearning to come to the Eucharist. Desire to possess Me wholly and to be entirely possessed by Me. Feed your desire by meditating on the wonder of the Eucharist. But if at times you feel no desire do not worry. The very wish to have it will suffice.

Come also with selflessness. I exist in the Eucharist to be a continuing love offering to My Father. Although the physical offering on Calvary could be made but once, the spiritual renewal can be repeated times without number. As I renew My love sacrifice, join yourself to Me and in union with Me offer to the Father *your* body and blood, *your* mind and spirit, *your* whole being, asking nothing for yourself, wanting only to give.

Above all, come with love. How often you receive Me thoughtlessly, mechanically. How often My priests hold Me in their hands carelessly. As the bread becomes infinitely noble in being changed into My body, so you must lovingly will to rise to infinitely noble life in and through Me. Give yourself to

Me so that I may transform you as if you were no more; so that henceforth you may be lost in the divinity; so that My Body may be your body, My Spirit your spirit, My acts your acts, My thoughts your thoughts; My love of the Father, your love of Him.

Come to the Eucharist with desire, with selflessness, with love, and I will do the rest. Then, indeed, you will live no more merely you, but I will live in you and you will live in Me.

— — — —

More than this, you will live in the Trinity.

Not only will you be one with Me in body and spirit, My other self, you will also be one with Him Who *is* My Spirit.

He dwells in Me in a complete union. Like the blood that flows from your heart into your arteries and through them into all your organs and members, the Holy Spirit—the Spirit of Love—My Spirit Who fills My Eucharistic body—flows from that body into you.

Uniting Himself with you, He makes you one spirit with Him as completely as you are the Body with Me.

You become one also with My Father Who receives you as His own. How can He do otherwise when you are so closely united with His Word? Can He spurn Me?

Or can He refuse to take you to Himself when He sees your spirit aflame with the very Person of Love Who proceeds from Him and Me?

Never! Through the Eucharist you offer Him the same Love —the Holy Spirit—which He receives from Me, His Son and Equal, in the Trinity. And He responds by showering on you the very Love—again the Holy Spirit—which He gives to Me.

The Eucharist, then, is the seal of your union with the Almighty. Because of your one-ness with Me you are joined also to the Father and the Holy Spirit in a unity which can be surpassed only by that face to face vision of the One WHO IS that will be yours in the life to come.

The Eucharist, indeed, is the pledge that this vision will be yours—for if anyone eats of this bread he shall live forever.

Why otherwise would I transform you into Me; why call you to such intimacy here on earth unless to prepare you for an even deeper intimacy hereafter?

My Body that nourishes you in the Eucharist is now hidden under a veil. In the fullness of the life to come that veil will be removed.

Then I will enlarge your capacity to receive the Divine Vision so that you will grasp and behold the Eternal One as He is in His own nature.

You will delight in the face to face sight and love of your Maker, your Sanctifier, your other Self.

You will be "in" your God totally, as a drop of water is in the ocean.

VII/AIDS TO AWARENESS

PRAYER

*". . .go to your room, close
your door and pray to your
Father in private" (Matt. 6:6).*

Eearlier we spoke of some obstacles to awareness which you
may meet. Now let us examine some of the means to overcome
these obstancles.

Do you remember the parable of the farmer who goes out
to sow his seed? As he sows, some falls close to the footpath
where it is trampled down or else the birds eat it up.

Other seed falls on stony ground, and as soon as it sprouts
it withers away because it can get no moisture.

Still other seed falls among thorns, and the thorns grow
up along with it and choke it.

But some seed falls on the right kind of soil, and it sprouts
and bears fruit a hundredfold.

I have begun to sow in you the seed of awareness of the
Divine Presence. But whether it will bear fruit depends on
how earnestly you cultivate the basic attitudes on which your
growth in awareness will rest.

The first of these attitudes is prayerfulness.

In one who lacks the habit of prayer, the seed indeed lies
on the footpath where it is easily lost.

To become *habitually* aware of Me you must be *frequently*
aware of Me in prayer. What is prayer but a *being aware of
Me*, whether by word, or thought, a mental glance or a kind
of breath of your soul?

What kind of prayer? All kinds, but especially mental
prayer, in which you retire within ycurself and silently come
to know Me better.

How few practice mental prayer. Many are unwilling.
Others pretend they do not know how or that they have no

need to pray. Even those who claim to love Me often give mental prayer a low priority. We want to pray, they say, but we seem to have neither time nor place.

They rise in the morning, they dress, they primp, they talk, they listen to the music and news on radio and television. But they have no time for Me.

While breakfasting they bury their minds in the newspaper, their attention swallowed by the passing parade of events, the "comics," sports, the crossword puzzle. They have no time for Me.

They may plunge into their tasks as though these were ends in themselves; or if they give their work only casual attention, their minds are filled with idle thoughts, day-dreaming, or conversation. They have no time.

The mid-morning "break" they occupy with gossip or light talk. Lunchtime: more conversation, rescanning the newspaper, finishing the puzzle, reading a novel, sometimes, "shop talk." But no time. The afternoon: business as usual, telephoning, meetings, another recreational break, more gossip and trivialities.

The precious evening leisure hours are devoured by escape reading, staring at the television, partying, the movies, or other more or less inconsequential pursuits. No time!

Their whole day has gone by in being acted upon, in responding to exterior stimuli. The seed has fallen on the footpath.

Is this true of you, My other self? Every day I give you roughly 1,000 minutes of wakefulness. Can you not share with Me in silent communion 30, 15, 10 minutes out of 1,000.

I know your work demands much of you. I know your need for recreation and socializing. But no time for mental prayer? Don't you see, you do not have time enough *not* to pray?

By failing to retire within yourself, there to seek and find Me, to taste joy and peace, to discover the truth that will make you free, you unthinkingly become a slave. You go in whichever direction events propel you. You surrender your opportunity to plan and choose how *you* will apply your time and efforts.

Regular mental prayer changes this. It permeates all your activities with a spiritual quality. It recalls the essential purposes of life. It helps you wisely apportion your time and energy among all your activities. It enables you to resist enslavement whether by recreation, pleasure or work. You determine in a rational manner how you shall employ your hours and talents in pursuit of objectives you have chosen. To save time is by no means the primary purpose of mental prayer; yet a few minutes of such prayer can add hours to your day.

If you would know Me intimately, you must set aside time for silent mental prayer every day. This is the only safeguard against the atrophy of spiritual muscle which preoccupation with worldly affairs brings on.

Augustine said, "As the fish cannot live without water, so that it languishes and dies when out of this element, so the soul cannot live without prayer, and when prayer is wanting, the soul begins to pine away."

Think of this seriously, My other self. If you do not give to silent mental prayer the time that you should, then start today. Not tomorrow, but this very day.

At first, your prayer will be meditative. You will simply think prayerfully about God or the things of God. After a time (weeks or months), you may find that you cannot reflect and reason as before. You will simply want to look at your God, to rest in Me.

You are being readied for higher forms of prayer; for prayer in which you wait on Me with a kind of passivity, a profound quiet, making no effort to reason, to imagine, to understand, but gently loving your God with a peaceful will.

What an unimaginable blessing it is that I permit you to pray thus. Listen again to Augustine. "Is it not astonishing that man, mere dust and ashes, should be admitted to a divine audience."

Not only do I admit you, I urge you and wait for you and

pledge you the most marvellous blessings, as if I, not you, were the gainer. "HOW DEEP ARE THE RICHES AND THE WISDOM AND THE KNOWLEDGE OF GOD! How inscrutable his judgments, how unsearchable his ways" (Romans 11, 33).

How foolish and ungrateful you would be not to love prayer and give it a place of honor in your daily life.

The way of prayer is the shortest road to the habitual awareness of My presence. More, unless you travel it, you will never reach the goal.

So begin at once, and persevere.

Do not, I beg you, permit the precious seed to lie on the footpath.

FAITH

"...if you had faith the size
of a mustard seed..."
(Matt. 17:20).

Some persons receive the message with joy, but do not let it strike root. The seed withers away because it lacks the moisture of a lively faith.

To enjoy a loving awareness of Me, My other self, you must prepare a place for Me by faith; or as Paul expressed it, "you must . . . acquire a fresh, spiritual way of thinking" (Eph. 4, 22-23).

It will be through faith, not through sensation or feeling, that you will know My presence. Feelings, emotions, sensations can deceive you. You must go the way of faith.

You know from the Gospels how I made faith prerequisite for those who asked My help. A leper approaches Me, throws Himself on the ground at My feet, pleading, "If you will, You can make me clean."

"Yes," I answer. "I am willing—be clean."

A centurion begs Me to heal his servant lying paralyzed at home. I test his faith. "Am I to come and cure him?" And when he replies, "I am not fit to have You come under my roof. No, only utter a word," what can I reply but, "Your wish shall be granted?"

Jairus implores Me to go with him to cure his 12 year old only daughter who is dying. Then a messenger comes to tell Jairus that his daughter is dead. I say to him, "Only have faith and she shall be safe." And I give her back to him.

Two blind men follow Me, calling "Take pity on us." When they enter after Me even the place where I am staying, I ask them, "Do you believe that I can do this?"

"Yes," they reply.

And I respond, "In answer to your faith, your wish shall be granted."

In the presence of faith the one word I cannot say is, "No."

That is why I pledged to My disciples, "You will receive anything you ask in your prayer provided you have faith."

Faith is sight, and to see by faith, My other self, is a far greater thing than to see with your eyes. Do you recall how I gave sight to the man blind from birth? A great gift, yes, but a greater was still to come. I sought him out, after the Pharisees had expelled him from the synagogue because of his honest answers to their malicious questions, and I asked him pointblank, "Do you believe in the Son of God?"

"Who is He?" he asked in turn.

"You are looking at Him. It is He who is now speaking to you."

"I do believe, sir," and he fell on his knees before Me.

I tell you that this "sight" of faith which I bestowed on him was more precious by far than the sight of his eyes which I had given him earlier.

Say to Me often, therefore, "My God, I believe that You are truly present in me. Increase my faith. Make your presence real to me. Lord, that I may see!"

You *must* do this. Beg for a strong and living faith.

Ask Me to enlighten you, to enliven you, to speak to you through faith so that you may begin to know Me as I really am.

Ask and pray. Pray the Creed, My other self. Pray it daily. Pray it slowly, meditatively, dwelling on its meaning.

Believe in God your Father—all powerful—all knowing—eternal—everywhere present. *Believe* that He made out of nothing all creation, visible and invisible, and that if He withdrew His will, all things, from the greatest star to the most microscopic worm would vanish instantaneously into nothingness.

Believe in Me, one Lord, Jesus Christ, the only-begotten Son of the Father—born of Him in eternity—God of God—Light of Light—true God of true God—of the same nature as My Father. *Believe* that the Word became flesh—that for you and your salvation I took flesh from a virgin girl by the action of the Holy Spirit, becoming a Person with two natures—making you co-heir with Me to everlasting glory.

Believe in the Holy Spirit—that He is Lord and giver of life—that He proceeds from the mutual love of My Father and Me—and that He possesses the same power and receives the same adoration and glory within the Trinity. *Believe* that He spoke through the prophets and that He guides and protects you today, and makes you holy by His power.

Believe that the providence of your God extends universally so that nothing can happen outside His plan—that all is in His hands, foreseen and provided for, and not one event is the result of blind chance.

Pray the Creed, and believe it, and ask for a boundless faith.

I do not force faith upon you. But eventually I will demonstrate truth in the supernatural world—and you will know the truth in the life to come.

Accept it now. Nourish it. Open your mind to it—the truth that makes you free—the faith that is life.

Happiness is yours, and peace, and joy, and all that the human heart has ever craved; if only you have faith. Do not let the seed wither away on stony, faithless ground.

Oh, My other self, it is through faith alone that you will know Me in this life, even though faintly, as I am. Live, then, by faith. Do this humbly and, on My word as God, I will, in My good time, reveal Myself to you.

SILENCE

*"I have stilled and
quieted my soul..."*
(Ps. 131:2).

Often the seed is choked by the cares of the world. This is why, besides prayerfulness and faith, My other self, you need to develop an attitude of silence. You cannot be aware of Me unless you listen to Me. My voice is quiet, and the noises of the world can drown it out. Only in stillness can you hear what I say to you.

What does it mean to have an attitude of silence? It does not mean becoming a hermit. Nor does it entail cutting yourself off from normal social contact, reasonable recreation, light, amusing conversation, or retiring behind your newspaper at breakfast.

You are not to be glum, downcast, sour, unfriendly, churlish. Listen to Thomas, "It is against reason for a man to be burdensome to others by offering no pleasure to others, and by hindering their enjoyment."

And listen to Philip Neri. "Cheer up! It's easier to be good when you are cheerful than when you are down-hearted."

Note that I emphasize not actual silence but an *attitude* of silence. Yet some actual silence is necessary to develop the attitude. Your first step toward silence is your period of mental prayer. But you need also to practice exterior silence by withdrawing into yourself from time to time for simple reflection, quiet reading, or repose.

You recognize your need for recreational breaks in your work routine. Recognize also the need for reflective and spiritual breaks. Now and again, even in the midst of your duties, seek a few moments of solitude to recollect My presence within you.

You must be in the world without pouring yourself out on the world.

You can exercise yourself in silence, even when you are not alone. You ought to take a normal part in conversation, including attentive listening, according to your capacity to contribute. But you need not always be the life of the party. Nor must you always blurt without deliberation the first thought or retort that leaps to your mind. Hold back a comment. If you are especially quick and glib, can you not curb yourself occasionally so as to permit others sometimes to be first with the bon mot?

Practice silence, then, in a reasonable, calm way; but do not forget to practice it.

So doing, you will gradually acquire an attitude of silence which will help you to master your time and energies and lead you to a growing awareness of My presence.

Even more important, however, is interior silence.

Just as the world is filled with needless noise, so you are likely to be afflicted with useless thoughts, imaginings, and memories, leaping up and down, running with uncontrolled abandon throughout the reaches of your mind, shouting, screaming, gesticulation, clamoring for attention.

If such is your state, there is no silence.

Anything that fills you with tension or anxiety; unrest resulting from ridicule or expressions of low esteem by your fellowmen; excessive striving for praise; too much attention to other persons' business; being in love with your own opinions—all these are noises of the spirit.

One of your essential spiritual duties, then, is continually to quiet yourself interiorly.

A man at peace makes his journey with ease and safety, while the tense and disquieted man can do nothing well and very quickly begins to fall back from weariness and discontent.

Sometimes a ruinous disquiet stems from unfulfilled ambitions. Guard against this poison, My other self. You can give Me only what I give you to give Me. What I desire is not the realization of your ambitions, noble as they may be, but the fulfillment of My unique plan for you. I am better satisfied to have you serenely dedicate yourself to some lowly occupation in accordance with My plan, than I could ever be even if you rose to the highest position in the nation simply to satisfy your self-inspired ambition.

You cannot expect to have an awareness of My presence when your mind is tense, anxious, full of unrest for position, prestige, or power. There is no room for Me in that inn.

Be on guard! Whenever you feel yourself troubled by disquiet, ask Me to help you quiet your soul.

At such times be especially deliberate in your actions. For example, when you are tempted to anger or impatience, slow your actions and your answers.

But how, you ask, can I achieve interior silence in the midst of today's turmoil? How can I remain calm under pressure? How can I be serene when I am pushed constantly to do this, do that, hurry up, don't delay, go faster? You must learn to see in every event and circumstance the presence of the Almighty. We will say more about this a little later.

For now be content with this thought. So long as you love Me, *all must work for your good.* Everything that comes to you or touches you reaches you through Me.

In time of war dispatches sometimes proclaim, "Everything is proceeding according to plan." Let this be your serenity: That where I am concerned if you but love Me, everything indeed proceeds according to plan—My plan for your joy.

Knowing this, you can afford to be calm, serene and silent even though your surroundings are in turmoil.

PURITY OF INTENTION

"Blessed are the single-hearted"
(Matt. 5:8).

When the seed falls on the right kind of soil, in those who listen to the message in the proper spirit and hold it fast, it bears abundant fruit.

Such are those who add to prayer, faith, and silence, true purity of heart.

Blessed are the pure of heart, My other self, for they shall see God.

Who are the pure of heart? Are they those who live chaste lives, who rule their flesh rather than allowing the flesh to rule them? Most assuredly, purity of heart requires this. But it requires more.

To be pure of heart is to be single-hearted.

It is to desire My will so completely that this attitude permeates your whole being.

He who, forgetting himself, seeks Me with a saintly simplicity of intention; who is so free of domination by the desire for wealth that he scorns to lay up treasures on earth; who abandons everything human that would lead him away from the divine; he is single-hearted. And he shall see God.

He shall see Me face to face in eternity. But even on this earth, he shall know My presence within him because he has turned his back on all else to turn his face to Me.

The essence of purity of heart is a profound forgetfulness of self.

How easy it is even for the good to permit self to be too much with them. Let Me illustrate. You make a special effort to worship at Mass on weekdays, and this pleases Me very much. But if you are not on guard, you may begin to take pride in your "holiness." You may look down your nose at others who do not do likewise.

Thus does self-love intrude upon the purity of your intention.

You may be a frequent communicant, and it delights Me to join Myself to you in this closest of all unions possible on earth. But one day you may find yourself boasting of your presence at the communion rail, smugly assuming that you are better than those not there. Self-praise has adulterated your once pure intention.

You may give alms, and again your intention may be pure. But if your vigilance fails, you may discover in yourself the faint counterpart of the rich Pharisee who stood in the temple returning thanks that he was not a sinner like the rest of men, that he fasted twice a week and gave tithes of all he possessed.

How much better to be humble and selfless, to fix your mind on your unworthiness, saying as did the publican, "O, God, be merciful to me a sinner."

What I ask of you, My other self, is the simple, pure intention of doing My will, unadulterated by pride and smug self-love. That is why the widow's mite found such favor with Me; because, forgetting herself, she gave with purity of heart.

To forget yourself is to reject all desires that build a barrier between us; renouncing sin, of course, but more than this, rejecting every wilful imperfection.

It is praying sometimes when you have no taste for prayer. It is regulating your appetites, perhaps giving up a particular delicacy at table to combat a too tender attachment to food; or foregoing a favorite recreation, a television program, or cutting down on light reading and idle conversation when you are becoming too attached to these diversions. It is to impose reasonable mortifications on yourself to insure that you remain captain of your soul.

To turn your back on yourself in this way can be easy or almost impossible. It is almost impossible so long as you strive to do it through your own efforts. It is easy when you place your hand in Mine and ask Me humbly to give you the desire and determination to do, as well as you can, everything for My love.

Let Me help you empty your heart of all unworthy desires, My other self. Let Me fill it with the one pure desire of doing everything for Me.

To test your single-heartedness there is a question you will need to ask yourself very frequently: "Why? Why am I doing this?" Strive to be able to answer: "I do it for you, Lord, not for praise, not to impress anyone, not even because I enjoy it; but because it is your will.

"I would do it if I were totally alone, with no one to see Me, if no one but You, Lord, were ever to know of it."

Again, I must assure you that this does not mean abjuring normal human sentiments. You have been asked, let us say, to participate in some outstanding event. You know that if you do well you will be highly praised and honored. How are you to keep your intention pure?

Simply resolve to do your best *for Me*, leaving the result in My hands, seeking neither praise nor honor, but accepting them if they come as My gifts. While thanking Me for My gifts, do not seek *them*, but only Me, the Giver Himself.

Strive for self-forgetfulness and a pure heart especially in prayer. Test yourself—what are you doing, and why? You are joining your feeble voice to the vast choir of angels and archangels, thrones and dominions, all the heavenly hosts, and all persons of good will in praise of the All-holy.

Would you pray if it gave you no pleasure? Would you do it simply because it is My will, because it pleases and glorifies the all-good God? Yes? That is self forgetfulness. This is a pure prayer.

Eventually you will have ever in your mind as I had ever in Mine the thought, "Father, what will you have me to do? Speak, Lord, your servant listens."

VIII / THE LORD IS HERE

BE WHAT YOU ARE

*"From heaven the Lord
looks down; he sees all
mankind"* (Ps. 33:13).

In the long history of the universe all has its place. Every blade of grass fulfills its purpose; every bird and beast, every fish, every worm does likewise. And each person, too, has his place.

In the sweep of human history, you have a purpose. It is slight proportionate to the whole; yet it is real, and in My Father's sight and in relation to your happiness, it is vastly important.

Each morning, then, poses for you the question: "What must I do this day?" and the true answer is, "Carry out your role in the divine plan as best you can. Serve your purpose in the whole of history as it is given to you on this particular day."

In practice this means faithfully carrying on your normal workaday routine: loving and serving your God, loving and serving your brothers, doing your work, staying cheerful, being kind, maintaining a serene mind and peaceful soul, being quick to help others, being vigilant lest you hurt anyone in word, act, or by neglect and omission.

You are to live "normally," as I did throughout almost all of My mortal life.

My life was so normally human that those who saw Me found it hard to credit that I was anyone other than the "son of Joseph the carpenter." They had a false notion of how a God-man would live.

After My public life had begun with My first signs and wonders, even My disciples did not penetrate My secret. Only later did Peter blurt out the truth revealed to him by My

Father, "You are the Christ, the Son of the living God." And only after I had risen from the tomb did Thomas speak for all in his salutation of awed faith, "My Lord and my God!"

Why was that? It was because for nearly all of My life, I did nothing except what was normal, so that no one had reason to see in Me more than humanity. Even the miracles I performed were surrounded and enveloped by thousands of normal everyday actions.

God walked the earth, but people saw in Him only a man. Yet I acted on earth as a God-Man would act. Kindness, faithfulness to duty, the preservation of serenity and love, *love*, LOVE—these are the characteristics of God-Made-Man. Normalities!

Is this what I wish from you after you have been given the precious gift of awareness? Yes.

Perhaps you also have a false notion of how one blessed with the gift of the divine awareness should live and act, and speak, and think.

You, who are My other self, are to live in awareness of the Divine Presence within you, yet almost nobody will know it or understand it. No matter. Guided by the Holy Spirit living in you, you will do as I did. You will be kind. You will be faithful in discharging your daily duties. You will preserve serenity because you walk with your hand in the hand of God. And you will love the Father, and your neighbor, and all God's works as they are manifested in the entire universe He has made. Normalities!

You are to be completely what you are.

What a wonderful thought it is that the eternal God has marked out for you a precise place of your own in His divine plan In you He sees something individual, something desirable, that does not exist in exactly the same way in any other person, not even in My own Mother.

What I ask of you is that you give back to Me, as completely as you are able, what I have first given you. I ask you to follow the road to holiness which corresponds to your unique nature and the particular circumstances of your life.

This is the milieu in which you are to seek your perfection.

So I say again: Strive to be completely what you are. This means accepting with the fullest consent of your will—as you did in your Act of Consecration—your present state in life, your personality with all your physical and mental equipment, your general health, your assets and liabilities. These are what you have from Me. These are what you have to give back to Me.

Being completely what you are means living what you are to the full; really trying to be the best husband and father, wife and mother, priest or sister, boy or girl you can; really trying to be the best employer or employee you can; really trying to be the best neighbor or parishioner or citizen you can.

It means not being content to live your life at half capacity, like a car chugging up a hill with half its cylinders misfiring.

Are you *really trying* to be the unique somebody I made you to be?

Some great churches contain huge and beautifully compelling mosaics of "the Christ" looking down on worshippers and visitors alike. Each piece in the mosaics is different. Each is ordered to contribute a certain color, shape or background to the whole design. This piece reacts to light so as to reflect redness; this one, blueness; this one, yellowness; this, purpleness; this, brownness.

So it is with you. You are to reflect the light of My presence in your own precise manner.

You are a piece of My Father's mosaic of THE CHRIST.

FIND ME IN YOUR WORK

"...*take courage,*
says the Lord, and work!
For I am with you" (Hag. 2:4).

You will more easily find Me in your occupations if you have a clear vision of the real meaning and role of work.

You must give work neither too large nor too small a place

in your life.

Some persons succumb to the temptation to make work everything. Success on the job is their number one concern. God, wife, husband, children, health: all are outranked by the compulsive need to get ahead in their careers.

For others, work is such drudgery it sets their teeth on edge. They are ground down by monotony. It's "blue Monday" at the beginning of the week and "Thank God it's Friday" at the end.

Still others regard work as a necessary evil which neither absorbs their attention nor arouses repugnance. Work is just a boring necessity which interferes with living; and living, for them, is what they do when they are not working.

But work is *good*. It is the opportunity I give you to help carry forward creation.

You tend to think that I am interested only in how you keep the Commandments and how you pray, not in your work. But I am intensely interested in how you perform your daily tasks. Indeed, I am your ultimate Employer.

There are certain things I ask of you as you carry out your duties. When you understand what they are, your work becomes more meaningful and you see its true role in your life.

First, you are to see your work in the context of the whole human family.

It is expected to contribute to the welfare of that family. You are not just carting stone from a quarry; you are helping to build the cathedral of a better world. You are furthering creation. No matter how unimportant, how menial, your position may seem, try to regard it as contributing to the sum total of human development. It is not without meaning that an employer sometimes says, "The most important people in this building are the secretaries."

You can "sanctify" your work by offering it to Me and doing it for Me. This is good and profitable. But it is even better to permit your work to sanctify you. This means viewing it as My gift to you, seeing in it My hand, hearing in it My voice, knowing that in it is My love. This is the work I give you for your sanctification. You do not have to sanctify it; this would be your action; you have only to accept it and perform it as My means of sanctifying you.

As you form the habit of dwelling in My presence you will find yourself doing this; not only referring everything to Me, but knowing that I am, in a sense, *in* your work; that I referred it to you. You will be less eager to put yourself into your work and more eager to find Me in it. As John the Baptist said, you must decrease, I must increase. This is true of your whole life, all your actions, words and thoughts. In all of them I must take an ever greater part, and your will, your desires, your selfishness, ever a smaller part.

The second demand I make of you is not that you succeed but that you do your reasonable best. You are to do your tasks with care and diligence but not with anxiety or worry. I would have you work calmly, peaceably, doing one thing at a time, not striving to do everything at once. I do not want your work to make you cross. Remember, I admonished Martha because she was troubled about her work—not because she was busy or diligent, but because she was "troubled" that Mary was not helping her.

Work calmly and perseveringly, not in a frenzy to finish, not allowing yourself to become troubled or upset.

Before you begin a task, say to Me: "Help me to do this as You wish it done. Help me to work through You, in You, and for You. Guide my thoughts and my actions and accept what I do as a gift of my love."

Say something like this—or think it—or let it be encompassed in a glance of your heart. Then begin.

As you work, I will call your mind to Me from time to time. Say a word to Me. Renew your intention. Again, a mere glance of the heart may be enough.

When you finish, turn to Me again. Look back over what you have done. If you have done it well, thank Me. If poorly, tell Me simply, "I'm sorry," and quietly resolve to do better next time. Then with peace of heart go on to your next duty or occupation.

This is the secret; doing your work with Me so that it speaks to Me of your love and to you of My love.

There will be times when you will approach the day's tasks with dread and foreboding, with distaste, even with disgust. You will awaken in the morning and you will wonder how you can possibly bring yourself to do all that awaits you, how you can hold yourself to the mark, how you can "get through" the dull, tasteless, irritating, enervating, devouring events that await you.

Turn your thoughts to Me for a moment. I know your feelings. I know your distaste, your foreboding and dread. Listen to what I say to you: This day that you are now beginning I have given to you not for your misery, but for your opportunity. Do not fear it. In your will, if not in your emotions, try to welcome it. Thank Me for giving you the gift of life this day. Say to Me, "Lord, help Me live this day as you wish Me to."

Your work, too, I know in every detail. Acknowledge that I have permitted it to come to you—*because under all the circumstances it is best at this time.* Say to Me, "Lord, I accept these tasks from Your Hands. You permit them; therefore I *will* them. But help Me."

I *will* help you. You need only do your best. I want nothing more. Do your best and *do not worry about the results.* And even though it may seem that I am letting you fail, believe Me, this failure will prove eventually to be your great success.

So go to your work, willingly, without fear, with confidence. *I am with you.* I will make it come out right.

Since I love you and think only of your welfare, these tasks must have in them seeds of great good for you. Perhaps all I ask is that you do not run away from them. Duties that may seem a hopeless maze may suddenly open into clear and easy paths for you to follow. Trust Me, I am with you.

The third thing I ask is that you remember that the worth of your work, like the worth of a gift, is measured by the love which prompts it.

Love is everything. That is why My saints have said that to

pick up a pin for the pure love of God is a greater deed than to preach a brilliant sermon for the love of praise and honors.

Therefore, the mother in the kitchen, the secretary in the office, the clerk in the store, the policeman on the beat, the teacher in the school can give Me gifts of work as great as those of presidents or prime ministers or kings—and even greater gifts if their love is purer than that of presidents, prime ministers, and kings.

There is no necessity for you to change your work, only to change your way of doing it. Do it no longer for human praise and reward, but because it is the task I have given you, the task I wish to do with you.

As I asked Joseph, My foster father, to allow Me to share in his carpentry, so I ask to be allowed to share in your labor.

My saints have found no more effective way of becoming perfect than by doing their daily tasks, so far as possible, not for human motives but for love of me.

Work performed with all your love can carry you to the pinnacle of sanctity.

AND IN SUFFERING

*"I believed even when
I said, 'I am greatly
afflicted'"* (Ps. 116:10).

You must learn to find Me even in suffering, My other self.

Suffering visits every life. It may come as physical pain: illness, ailments, accident. It may come as worry: financial problems, threats to your job or property, the fear of failure in business or your profession. It may come as a saddening disappointment: discord at home, a son or daughter rejecting family or faith, throwing away opportunities at school, becoming addicted to drugs or drink. It may come as grief: helplessly standing by while a little child, a parent, a brother or sister, a wife or husband slowly dies; or seeing metal illness corrode the mind of one you idolize.

Suffering has come to you. It will come again. And you

must be able to find Me in it.

When you are in the grip of suffering you ask: Why? Why must suffering be our common lot and why is it so inescapable?

Because it is *the test*, My other self.

It is easy for you to think you love Me when all your days are filled with joy. Obedience that costs nothing tests nothing. It is only along the way of the cross and on Calvary that you prove yourself.

Yet suffering is more than a test. It is a reminder that this mortal life is not your *real* life, nor this earth your permanent home.

But above all, suffering is the hammer and chisel of holiness. Though it is not good in itself, something wonderfully good can be derived *from* it. As a Michelangelo chisels out the beauty hidden in a block of marble, so your Father uses suffering to bring out the exact measure of beauty and heroism He has implanted in you. A Master Sculptor, He knows exactly how hard to let the hammer strike.

He knew exactly how hard to strike Paul, who confesses in his second letter to the Corinthians: "That I might not become conceited, I was given a thorn in the flesh."

With awful precision He struck Mary's soul as she watched Me fall beneath the heavy cross, saw Me driven like an animal through the streets of Jerusalem, and witnessed My life's blood welling out of My pierced hands and feet.

It can only be because suffering is essential that My Father bestowed it upon My own human nature—and in such terrible measure.

Surely I know what I am doing when I permit you to suffer. Indeed, the more afflicting the suffering I permit you to endure, the greater must be My regard for you. Since I will not try you beyond your strength, it must follow that great trials are matched by great faith, great trust, great love, and great rewards.

Yet it is natural for you to be bewildered. You wonder: Can it truly be that suffering which hurts so much *must* work unto good if only you love God?

Why do a loving father and mother subject the child of their mutual love to the pains of surgery? Only for a greater good that can be obtained in no other way. And when the child is undergoing this painful ordeal, his parents provide encouragement, gifts, and extraordinary proofs of their love. Surely your Heavenly Father is no less versed in the medicine of love than you, whose love is but the palest reflection of His.

How many times parents make up to a child for a pain, a loss, a disappointment, an injustice, in ways that the child never recognizes, or perhaps recognizes only weeks, months, or even years later? Can your God do less? Surely, it must be true that when at last you see Him face to face, you will understand with a certain knowledge that He did indeed make all things work together for your good. Omnipotence has the power to make up whatever is lacking—and love demands that Omnipotence do so.

The cross of suffering is not something to be avoided. Neither, generally speaking, is it something to be sought. Rather, the cross is to be accepted, and borne, exactly as I present it to you at every present moment.

Whatever your cross and however burdensome it may be, it is intended to be a seed bed of virtue; and it *can* be. It is the key to holiness which I Myself hold out to you. Patiently, willingly, lovingly bear it, and you are in effect carrying a sliver, or more, of My cross. You are sharing in My atonement, making up as Paul put it "what is lacking in the sufferings of Christ."

When illness besets you; when your body cries for rest and there is no rest; when you are tormented by worry that seems beyond your power to control; when you are subjected to ridicule and have lost the respect of others; when grief assaults you and threatens to overcome you; when you feel momentarily that even your God has deserted you and your broken, abandoned spirit is totally unable to bear another wound, then let Me call to your mind as I did to Francis de Sales, sentiments such as these:

Your God in His divine wisdom
has from all eternity beheld the cross
He bestows upon you —
His precious gift
from His heart.

He contemplated this cross
with His all-knowing eye
before bestowing it upon you.

He pondered over it
with His divine mind;
He examined it
with His all-wise justice;
with His loving mercy
He warmed it through and through.

And with both His hands
He weighed it
to determine if it be
one ounce too heavy for you.

He blessed it with His all-holy Name.
With His grace He anointed it.
And with His consolation he perfumed it.

And then once more
He considered you
and your courage.

Finally, it comes from heaven
as a special message of God
to you;
an alms
of the all-merciful love of God
for you.

With such a sublime concept of the Divine Love is it any
wonder that Francis could say: "If jealousy could enter into
the realm of eternal love, the angels themselves would envy
the sufferings of God for man, and those of man for God?"

AND IN EVERY MOMENT

*"I will praise the Lord
all my life"* (Ps. 146:2).

I have shown you, My other self, how to grow in awareness through prayer, faith, silence, and purity of intention. And I have urged you to seek Me in your daily routine, your work, and even your sufferings.

But I desire even more of you and for you. You must learn to find Me in every present moment.

Understand that, in a sense, I "speak" to you at every instant through all that I permit to touch or happen to you. What I would have you do is to recognize My presence in every circumstance of the present moment and conform your will to Mine as this moment reveals it.

In this lies the holiness of My saints. Each expressed it in his own terms, but the core is a recognition and union of will with My designs at each present moment.

Paul spoke of praying without ceasing. Francis of Assisi expressed it in his concept of the brotherhood of all creation; Francis de Sales in his famous dictum, "desire nothing, refuse nothing"; Therese in her "little way."

Permitting Me to lead you moment by moment, recognizing with loving faith that whatever happens to you at each moment by My design is *best,* accepting the present moment in its totality: this is perfection.

Assuredly, this is true. It is so easily understood that you are likely to assume that it is equally easy to practice. It is not. On the contrary, it requires heroic perseverance.

While there are many who say, "Lord, I accept without reservation whatever You permit to happen to me," few are actually as good as their word. If you are to practice what you promise, you must strive to acquire a deep faith that I truly have foreseen, permitted, and even planned the circumstances of your entire life in every detail no matter how insignificant.

The sorrows, disappointments, and frustrations of your daily routine are not the result of blind chance. The monotony of your work, the drudgery of your household duties; this employer whose orders are so brusquely delivered, this supervisor whose criticism is so biting; this neighbor who gets in your way with misguided kindness, or that one who always seems to intrude on your privacy when you particularly want to be alone; all these offer opportunities for you to practice the acceptance of My will of the present moment—and opportunities to find Me in this moment.

Your headaches, backaches, toothaches; your fatigue, irritability, moodiness; your temptations, anxieties, fears; the insults, slights, ridicule you may have to endure—all these invite you to grow in awareness of My presence. The loving recognition that these little crosses have My mark on them is the essence of holiness.

What you would ordinarily consider not only worthless but even a hindrance to your spiritual growth can be the very means by which I speak to you and reveal Myself to you.

But it is not only your sorrows, frustrations, and pains which can bring you close to Me. Why is it that you think of "fiat—Your will be done" only in terms of crosses? When My Mother uttered her "fiat" it was in loving acceptance of the incomprehensible *joy* of her life—her becoming the Mother of the Most High.

Somehow you seem to regard your joys as things you have earned or that come to you automatically in the natural order of living. Only your sorrows, your crosses, especially the big and painful ones, come from Me.

Do not deny Me the "fiats" you owe Me for the joys I send. I want you to recognize these as My gifts, too.

"It is a beautiful day—fiat, and thank You, Lord."

"My work goes well—fiat, and thank You."

"Our children have received an honor—fiat."

"We are thrilled by the joys of marriage—fiat."

Your laughter at a joke, your pleasure at a movie, your relaxation in a game, your enjoyment of delicious food—these, too, are to be accepted, willed as coming from My hands, recognized as being part of My moment by moment plan for your perfection.

To acquire such an awareness that I speak to you in all that I permit to occur, it is necessary for you to meditate on this truth and from time to time during the day call to mind such thoughts as these: Lord, not only do I accept this moment with its exact and most minute circumstances, I *will* it because it is Your will.

Doing this is a source of deep spiritual peace. If you trust Me enough to make My will yours at each moment, you can afford to be gentle, unhurried, untroubled, serene. No longer does the universe need your hand on the throttle. No longer do you need to fret about what is ahead of you tomorrow or next year. You can afford to leave the future to Me.

This virtue called by many different names—self-abandonment, self-renunciation, conformity to the will of God, the little way—is the means whereby you become the unique person I wish you to be at any given moment.

True, to persevere in it requires great faith, great trust, and great love. But no sooner do you place yourself completely in My hands than I provide an answer to your every question, a remedy to every ailment, a solace for every cross, and assurance of My presence at every moment.

IX / THE DIVINE PLAN

YOUR *REAL* LIFE

*"...the life I live now is not
my own; Christ is living in me"* (Gal. 2:20).

Do you begin now to understand the divine plan? Do you glimpse how closely the mysteries of the Trinity, the Incarnation, and the Eucharist are related; how they make possible the divine indwelling; how, through them, divine life is given to you?

In the Trinity you see the Son of God in the bosom of the Father, united to Him through the Spirit of Love.

In the Incarnation you see the Son of God in the womb of an earthly mother, becoming the son of man so that you might become a son of God.

In the Eucharist you see the Son of God and son of man joining Himself to you in an overwhelming proof of the divine love. As My mother fed Me from her body making Me one with mankind, so I feed you with My body in a predominantly spiritual way, making you one with Me.

To sum it up: In the Trinity the Father pours Himself into His Son. In the Incarnation the Son pours Himself into a human nature. In the Eucharist I pour Myself into you.

And all this is done so that the limitless life and love of the Divine Being may flood out into creation—and that this same limitless living love may be returned to the ONE WHO IS. You, one speck in the universe, are united with all of creation in the Head of creation, the Eternal Word, the Son of the Father, so that you may join with Him in celebrating the life and love, the greatness and glory, of the ONE WHO IS—so that you may possess supernatural life, which is to know and love the Divine Being.

This was the mysterious design, hidden from man from the beginning, until My Father in the fulness of time sent Me to reveal it.

I have told you that superhuman life—that life which is above your human nature—is the highest life. But you still find it hard to grasp.

Because super-human life is spiritual, you tend to regard it as unreal, certainly as *less* real than your natural life.

Could I have made it plainer that super-human life is real and immeasurably superior to your natural life? Was it for an unreal life that I suffered death?

Was I speaking of an inferior life when I said: "I am the way, and the truth, and the *life*?... If you drink the living water that I will give, you will live forever... He who believes in Me possesses eternal life... He who follows Me will possess the light which is life... I am the resurrection and the life; he who believes in me though he is dead (in his natural life) will live on; and whoever has faith in Me, to all eternity cannot die."

Surely all this bespeaks a fullness of life far beyond the natural.

Paul understood this when he said, "The life I live now is not my own... it is a life of faith in the Son of God" (Gal. 2:20). He fathomed the meaning of my words, "What profit would a man show if he were to gain the whole world and destroy himself... What can a man offer in exchange for his very self?" (Matt. 16:26).

Understand this well, My other self, the superhuman life is a *real* life.

Do not think of it as a kind of an inferior appendage to your natural life, something that will become important later on but that is vague and shadowy and not quite real now.

How shallow and how constrained your human existence would be if you lived without love or friendship and with little knowledge or appreciation of literature and beauty. But far more would you be in bondage if you had no knowledge or love of your God. Without any real sense of morality, of your place in creation, of the unity and continuity of humanity, how narrow and mistaken would be your view of yourself, how purposeless your existence.

Small wonder that modern man does not dare to think of death, when it means oblivion. Small wonder that he clings desperately to youth, money, pleasure, when there is nothing else to look forward to.

These who see this world as all and who tell man that the highest ideal is to be something less than a saint, sell man short. They frustrate his highest development. They present a twisted, misshapen, grotesque view of man—like a figure in the "crazy mirror" at an amusement park.

The saint is man developed to the fullest. The poet, the artist, the sculptor seek to express beauty in word, or canvas, or marble. The saint seeks in his whole life to express God, the Author of beauty.

The poet or the artist gives his thought or his painting to others; the saint gives *himself* through his service to the Almighty One.

That supernatural life far surpasses the highest development of natural human life is evidenced by what happens to men and women when they become saints; the Curé of Ars, Augustine, Paul, the Apostles at Pentecost. How they were changed!

How far the saints outshine their fellowmen of great worldly achievement! Contrast the writings of Paul with those of Shakespeare. Which has had the greater influence, which has been the larger force for good, which has done more to inspire man to goodness, service, and love?

Or contrast Thomas Aquinas with Nietzche, Ignatius of Loyola with Napoleon, Francis of Assisi with Lenin.

Though the world is ephemeral, illusory, unfulfilling, it is so much with you that it is easy to make it everything. Learn of Augustine who said, "Restless are our hearts, O God, until they rest in You."

Just as natural human life becomes richer as you learn to love your fellowman, to use your reason, to appreciate literature, music and the arts, to write, compose, play music, paint, or sculpt, so also your supernatural life grows and deepens with your awakening knowledge and love of the Divine Being.

And just as natural human life is sometimes glowingly enriched by a sudden appreciation of literature, music, or beauty, so that one becomes a deeper, broader, livelier person, so also in the supernatural life I wish to arouse in you a suddenly deepened faith and love, and give you a new awareness of Me. Your eyes are opened and you are a different person.

Your existence turns on a new axis. Worldly goals, which formerly seemed almost ends in themselves, are now seen as secondary to and at best complementary to supernatural ends. Whereas before your ambitions may have been focussed on human glory and your energies directed toward achieving power, pleasure, or prestige, now your ambitions and energies are directed toward goals more sublime. You work and play and live much as before, but you do it all with a new outlook and for a new purpose.

This is because, in some way, you have encountered the ONE-WHO-IS and He has touched you, spoken to you, and conferred upon you a share in the Divine life itself.

With supernatural life comes enlightenment, the knowledge of what your God expects of you. With it comes humility, so that you see yourself increasingly as you really are. With it comes trust, so that while you recognize your utter dependence on the Divine Being, you have assurance that He will provide whatever you need.

This, then, is the super-human life—to know and love Me, and the Father Who sent Me, and the Spirit of Love whom I give to you.

But this life can exist in you on an infantile level or on the fully adult level—which is sainthood.

That you may be fully adult is My plan for you. Seek it. Seek to know and love the ONE-WHO-IS. Seek Him in all the ways I have opened up to you.

This is how you play your full role in the drama of creation. To help you do this is the purpose of My gift of awareness.

THE DIVINE LOVE

*"... the breadth and length
and height and depth
of Christ's love...
surpasses all knowledge"* (Eph. 3:18-19).

When you begin to see the divine plan, My other self, you understand that no man, no woman, no child lives now or ever lived who can say in truth: "I am alone and unloved. No one cares for me."

Even if all those around you ignored you, and no audible voice ever said, "I love you," even though not one person ever called you friend or showed you one act of kindness, still you could not truthfully say, "No one loves me" or "No one is in love with me."

The Divine Being Who holds the universe in existence by His will alone, He Who is the Reality from Whom all beings and all things take their reality, HE WHO IS—He loves you.

Yes, and more than this, speaking in your human terms, He is *in love with you.*

Far more is He in love with you than the most devoted husband and wife are in love with each other. The deepest, most consuming, most enveloping love of man for woman parent for child, friend for friend, is but a candle flicker beside the great searchlight of your God's "in-love-ness" with you.

The image of bride and bridegroom in Scripture that is employed to signify the union between the Divine Being and man is but a faint likeness of the real union with Him to which you are called.

Yet it is a true image. As the bridegroom is the leader in human love, so your God is the Leader in this love of which I speak. Even as the bridegroom seeks after his bride, so do I seek you. The human lover may become discouraged and stop his pursuit, but I shall continue to pursue you until finally you accept or reject Me at the instant your mortal life ends.

As in human love, the initiative is Mine, and I took it when from all eternity I saw you in My intellect (as a human lover sees Beauty across a room) and wanted you—wanted you enough to create you.

Think, My other self! think of a love so great that it calls for your *creation* to satisfy it.

Even as a human lover showers attention, gifts, joys upon his beloved, do I not take care of you, call you to Me, put Myself in your presence so that you will notice Me?

This I do not only through the glories of creation and the beauty of nature; but also through the joy and consolations I pour out on you in prayer so that you will speak to Me often.

I give you My Spirit of Love to be your own. More, I give you Myself in the Sacrament of Love, the final and most overwhelming proof of all on earth that *you* are important, that *you* are My beloved.

Human lovers give themselves to each other physically and emotionally, body and spirit. I give Myself to you, Body and Soul, Humanity and Divinity, holding back nothing but the face-to-face vision of the God-Man and My Father and the Spirit which can only be had in the final union of Heaven.

As the bride draws strength from her husband and glories in the arms of her beloved and feels secure and confident there; so you are to glory in Me. You are My beloved and I am your Protector. My strength is yours, My wisdom also. Place yourself in My care; have no fear. Nothing can touch you without My permission. And since I love you with the truest love of all, I will cause whatever happens to turn out "best" for you.

I want you for Myself. This is what is mean by the words, "a jealous God." Not wanting to share you with competing loves, I try to detach you from them, for to share you may be to lose you.

I want to be loved not for My gifts but for what I am—for Myself alone. So I test you in a way that no human would ever dare test his beloved. I withdraw My consolations in prayer to see whether you pray because it makes you feel good or because you love Me.

I seek to detach you from your material possessions, and in death I separate you from your friends and your family.

Do you love Me because of them, or do you love Me for Myself?

With divine wisdom, I guide your love, knowing exactly what will best make it grow: now gifts, now deprivations; now joys, now sufferings; feeding the fire of your love, a splinter when a splinter is best, a log when a log will burn most brightly.

Thus I nurture in you a perfect love; a love in which the will of your God becomes completely your will; His thoughts your thoughts; His desires your desires; until so far as it can be on earth your God and you are identified.

And so you will come at last, at the end of your mortal life, to the fulfillment of it all—to that joy above joy which only Divine Wisdom and Power and Goodness and Love could devise—that union above unions of which marriage is but the faintest shadow—the joy and union of the Vision of God Himself.

This is the divine plan—My plan—for you.

THE PLEDGE OF GLORY

"... O Lord, give me life
according to your word" (Ps. 119: 107).

And now we come to the last of these conversations, and it is fitting that we should speak about death.

Do you fear death, My other self? You do not need to fear it.

The Trinity, the Incarnation, and the Eucharist are guarantees that death is not the end of your life but your entrance into life's fulfillment. Why did I reveal the inner life of God if you are not to have some share in it? Why did I raise humanity so high by taking a human nature if death is to be the end? Why do I unite Myself to you in the Eucharist except as a pledge and a prelude to a more complete union that is to come?

In death My Father opens wide for you the door to His palace. Because you love Him He says to you: WELCOME!

I understand fully why you cringe at losing your dear ones. You don't want to be separated from them and you know that your death will cause them sorrow. It is appropriate to mourn the temporary separation from those we love. The saints weep at death's parting. Seeing Martha's and Mary's grief over the death of Lazarus, I also wept.

But this is not to fear death; it is simply to grieve over separation.

Because of your union with Me you do not go to your death as a punishment. You take it upon yourself, as I did, in loving submission to the Father. You trust that He will make it to come out right. And therefore death becomes for you a source of life. I have taken away its victory; I have removed its sting.

Your willing acceptance of death is your final gift of self, your ultimate surrender, your complete abandonment to the divine will.

And because of this gift of yourself, just as My body rose from the tomb and was transfigured into glory, so it must one day be with yours. As Paul said, "Christ is now raised from the dead, the first fruits of those who have fallen asleep. God will bring forth with Him from the dead those also who have fallen asleep believing in Him." The miracles of the Resurrection and the Transfiguration will be wrought in you also.

What, then, is death? It is a meeting place, a rendezvouz I have prepared where we shall meet with a kiss. It is the signature you and I together place on your mortal existence. It is not the end of life but a new beginning.

The awe-full truth, and I use the word in the sense of a truth which should fill you with awe, is that once I give you existence, your existence can never end. Once I create the spirit which inhabits your frail body, you go on forever. You cannot stop your existence. You cannot annihilate it. It is there as a continuing, unceasing, everlasting fact.

Don't you understand, My other self, that your life after death will outshine your present mortal life as your present life outshines that which you had in your mother's womb?

You had life in the womb—the same life you possess today. But not until after you were born did you begin to come into its fulness. Similarly, the life you shall possess when you come before your God is the same as the divine life you now possess —but, oh, how much more wonderful—how much more complete—how utterly perfect it will be!

You see now as in a mirror, darkly—but then you shall see your God face to face.

As the embryo was conceived for birth into life, so you have been baptized for birth into heaven. And as the new born babe leaves the womb to enter its more perfect existence on earth, so you leave this mortal existence to enter a new and unimaginably wonderful life in heaven. This is adventure. This is fulfillment. This is completion.

But perhaps you ask: "What is this life?" The idea of "eternal rest" is not too inviting. The rest you shall enjoy, My other self, is not inactivity; it is rest from turmoil, trouble, pain, hardship, illness, temptation, drudgery. It is the "rest" of serenity and peace.

The higher the scale of life, the more productive, creative and communicative it is. Am I not active in heaven? If I am not, why do you address your prayers to the Father in My Name?

Are the saints not active? Why, then, do you ask them to intercede for you? And how do you explain the miracles which are requisite for their canonization?

The fulness of life that will be yours after death is the continuation and perfection of the divine life you already enjoy.

Here on earth you see the divine plan vaguely as it relates to your own life—and you help carry it out. United to your God you will see the Divine Plan in its totality—and you will have a part in bringing it to fulfillment.

Here on earth you find a little circle of divine love. When you come to your God you will enter a community of divine love.

Here on earth you experience union with Me vaguely in the Sacrament of Love. There you will see Me and know Me and live in Me in a never-ending, fully-realized oneness.

Here you know the beginning of divine friendship. There you will experience the total friendship of the Trinity—and that of Mary and Joseph, Peter and Paul, and all the saints including your loved ones of earth.

Here you enjoy a taste of peace and harmony and oneness with mankind. There you will know the perfection of peace and harmony and oneness.

Here you begin to comprehend divine truth, to discover it. to recognize it. There you will be absorbed in Truth Itself—and the joy of discovery and the delight of knowledge will eternally be yours.

What then is the perfection of divine life? It is the joy of belonging completely to your God—of being joined to infinite Goodness—infinite Beauty—infinite Truth—infinite Love. It is knowing your God and in your knowledge of Him loving Him yet more; and in loving Him more, knowing Him yet better; and knowing Him and loving Him in an eternal spiral of knowledge and love that will complete your every desire.

If you but knew what I know about what awaits you after death, My other self, you would clap your hands for joy. For what has been prepared for you by a loving Father for your delight and His,

"eye has not seen, ear has not heard, nor has it so
much as dawned on man."

So it is for the pagan to say: "Eat, drink, and be merry, for tomorrow we die."

The attitude of those whom I call My other selves, is totally different. It is "PRAISE GOD, GIVE THANKS, AND BE JOYFUL—FOR TOMORROW WE LIVE!"